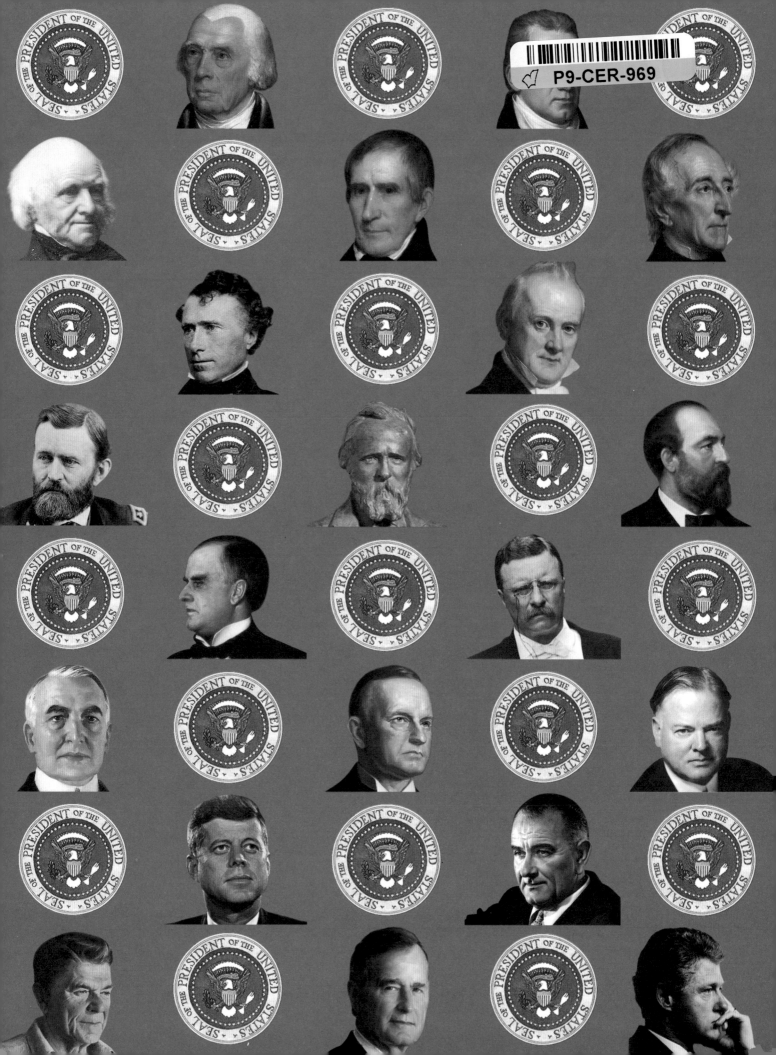

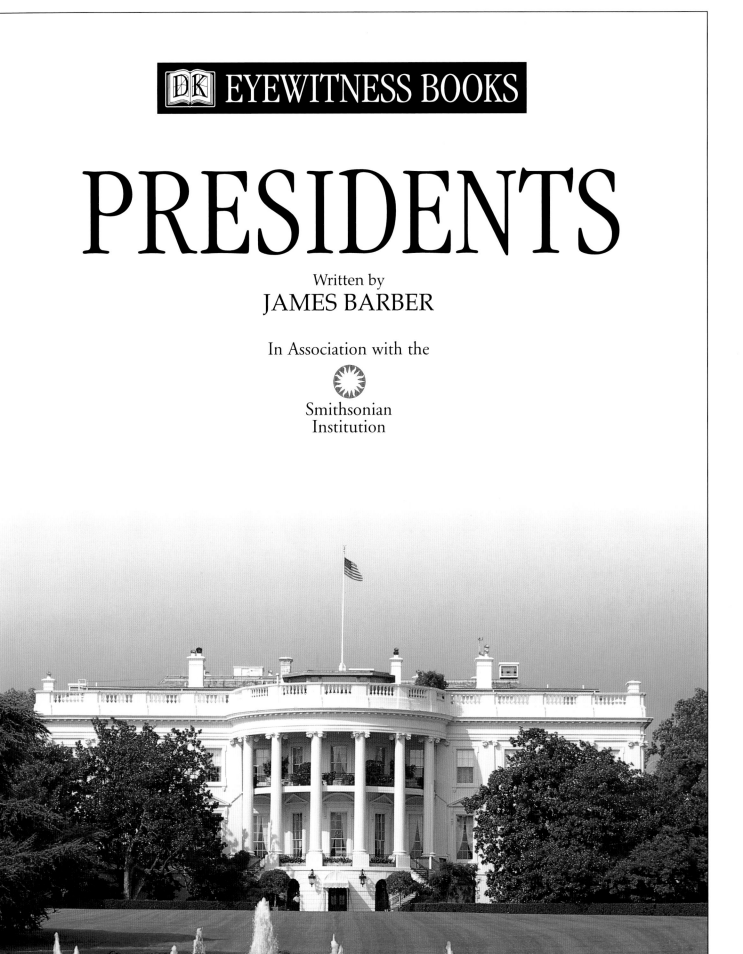

DK EYEWITNESS BOOKS

PRESIDENTS

Written by
JAMES BARBER

In Association with the

Smithsonian
Institution

Fan commemorating Lincoln

Theodore Roosevelt banner

Carter campaign memorabilia

Anti-Nixon buttons

McKinley campaign umbrella

Dorling Kindersley

LONDON, NEW YORK, AUCKLAND, DELHI, JOHANNESBURG, MUNICH, PARIS and SYDNEY

For a full catalog, visit

Created by Leapfrog Press Ltd
Senior Editor and Co-Author Bridget Hopkinson
Editor Jacky Jackson
Art Director Miranda Kennedy
Art Editors Catherine Goldsmith and Adrienne Hutchinson
Picture Researcher Liz Moore

For Dorling Kindersley Publishing, Inc.
Publisher Neal Porter
Executive Editor Iris Rosoff
Art Director Dirk Kaufman

First American Edition, 2000
2 4 6 8 10 9 7 5 3 1

Published in the United States by Dorling Kindersley Publishing, Inc.
95 Madison Avenue, New York, New York 10016

Dorling Kindersley books are available at special discounts for bulk purchases for
sales promotions or premiums. Special editions, including personalized covers,
excerpts of existing guides, and corporate imprints can be created in large quantities
for specific needs. For more information, contact Special Markets Dept./Dorling
Kindersley Publishing, Inc./95 Madison Ave./New York, NY 10016/Fax:800-600-9098.

Library of Congress Cataloging-in-Publication Data
Barber, James, 1952-
Presidents / by James Barber.— 1st American ed.
p. cm — (Dorling Kindersley eyewitness)
ISBN 0-7894-5243-X (HC) ISBN 0-7894-6242-7 (PB)
1. Presidents—United States—History—Juvenile literature. 2. Presidents—United
States—Biography—Juvenile literature. I. Title II. Series.

E176.1. B218 2000
973'.09'9—dc21   99-043281

Color reproduction by Colourscan, Singapore
Printed in China by Toppan Printing Co. (s) Pte Ltd.

Carter bumper stickers

Eyeglasses belonging to
James K. Polk

Life magazine cover from the
Coolidge era

Lewis and Clark compass from
Jefferson's presidency

Dance wand from the Cherokee tribe
(Jackson era)

Teddy bear named
after Teddy Roosevelt

Contents

Buchanan campaign flag

George Washington's field kit from the Revolutionary War

George Washington

Compass belonging to Washington

In 1789, George Washington was sworn in as the first president of the newly formed United States of America. The American colonies had won their independence from Great Britain in the Revolutionary War. Washington was the hero of the war and he was everyone's first choice to be president. He was "in every sense of the word, a wise, a good, and a great man," stated Thomas Jefferson (p. 10). Washington displayed wisdom and moderation in launching the new United States' government, which had much to accomplish before it could win the respect of nations such as Great Britain, France, and Spain. Americans had chosen their ideal leader. Washington's example defined the presidency for all time.

This is the military mess kit that George Washington carried with him in the Revolutionary War.

General Washington leads his troops across the Delaware River on Christmas Day, 1776

Revolutionary leadership

As a young man, George Washington was made commander of the colonial army in Virginia and fought in fierce battles against the French and the Indians. When the Revolutionary War against Britain began in 1775, Washington was chosen as commander of the American forces. He was not a great military strategist, but he had common sense and determination. Washington succeeded in holding his badly equipped army together and finally secured victory in 1781.

CROSSING THE DELAWARE
December, 1776, was one of the Patriots' darkest hours. Outmaneuvered and defeated by the British at Long Island in August, it seemed as though their cause was all but lost. But then General Washington struck a daring blow. On December 25, he led his 2,400-man army across the icy Delaware River under cover of darkness. Surprising the enemy, he won a vital victory at Trenton, New Jersey.

Patriot medal celebrating an early victory over the British at Boston, March, 1776

During the war, Washington would have spent long hours in this camp tent planning his next move against the British.

FORGING THE CONSTITUTION

In 1787, Washington presided over the Constitutional Convention in Philadelphia and helped draft a new system of democratic government. It had three branches, each of which was intended to exercise checks and balances over the others. The Senate and the House of Representatives would make the laws in the legislative branch, the Supreme Court would dispense justice in the judiciary branch, and the president would enforce the laws in the executive branch. Besides the central government, state and local governments would comprise the American system of democracy.

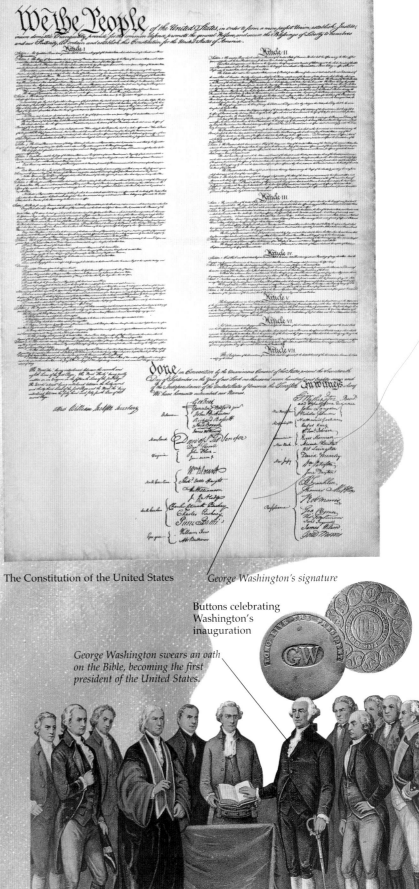

The Constitution of the United States

George Washington's signature

Buttons celebrating Washington's inauguration

George Washington swears an oath on the Bible, becoming the first president of the United States.

THE NEW PRESIDENT

George Washington's powers as president were set out clearly under the new constitution. It was his responsibility to make sure that the laws of the land were followed and to appoint high-ranking government officials and judges. He also had the power to command the armed forces and to make treaties with other countries. Washington was so admired by the people that he probably could have been president for as long as he wished. But the constitution stated that each president should serve a four-year term of office and then stand for reelection. Washington did this, and after two terms, he decided that he had served long enough.

5

Continued on next page

Washington at home

George Washington grew up on a farm near the Rappahannock River in Virginia. At the age of 20, he inherited the Mount Vernon estate and became one of the largest landowners in northern Virginia. He loved farming, regarding it as "the most noble employment of man." When at home, he filled his days attending to the running of his plantation and pursued such country sports as hunting and fishing. Much of his time in his last years was spent with his wife, Martha, entertaining the hundreds of guests who visited Mount Vernon every year.

Set of false teeth belonging to George Washington

Washington with his wife, Martha, and two of her grandchildren, c.1796

George Washington Parke Custis

Washington liked fine clothes and ordered most of his coats from London.

Eleanor Parke Custis

Martha Washington had a dignified bearing.

MOUNT VERNON
In his early years at Mount Vernon, Washington improved the house and gradually added new land to his estate until it covered over 8,000 acres. He experimented with new scientific ways of improving his crops and livestock, and he especially enjoyed planting trees, several of which still tower over the estate today.

MARTHA WASHINGTON
In January, 1759, George Washington married a wealthy widow, Martha Dandridge Custis. Although the couple remained childless themselves, Washington became father to Martha's two children from her first marriage. When Washington was elected president, Martha grew into her role of First Lady. She hosted the numerous official dinners and receptions with great decorum.

THE WHISKEY REBELLION
In 1794, Washington's authority as president was tested for the first time when a rebellion broke out in Pennsylvania. Farmers were angry about a new federal whiskey tax. The governor of Pennsylvania refused to enforce the tax, so Washington sent an army to make sure that the law was obeyed. His swift and decisive action left Americans in no doubt about the power of their new leader.

A federal officer tarred and feathered by angry farmers.

PRESIDENTIAL ENTERTAINING
George Washington believed that as the new president of the United States he should conduct himself with reserve and dignity, as befitted his station. He tended to be formal with colleagues and traveled in a splendid horse-drawn carriage. Dinners and receptions were also formal affairs, and guests referred to their hosts as President and Lady Washington.

INDIAN WARS

Conflict between white settlers and Native American tribes was a pressing issue for George Washington. When an army of U.S. troops was ambushed by Indians of the Northwest Confederation, Washington quickly sent more troops to support them. This time his army defeated the tribes at the Battle of Fallen Timbers. By the Treaty of Fort Greenville, 1795, the Indian Confederation was forced to give most of Ohio to the U.S. government.

SENECA CHIEF

Whenever possible, Washington was prepared to negotiate with tribal chiefs. In 1792, he met Chief Red Jacket of the Seneca tribe. Red Jacket had agreed to grant land concessions to the U.S. government, and Washington gave him a silver medal as a sign of his good faith.

U.S. officers at the Battle of Fallen Timbers, 1794

An early likeness of George Washington to appear in print, 1792

The legend of George Washington

George Washington became a legend in his own lifetime. He had endured the trials of fighting a war and forging a nation with courage and strength of purpose, and his virtues became associated with the character of the new republic. He was called the "Father of His Country" and his image soon began to appear on everything from porcelain to banknotes. After his death, the story of his life was retold and embellished by admiring writers and poets.

CHILDHOOD MYTH

In his *Life of Washington* (1806), Mason L. Weems described a legendary event from George Washington's childhood that he believed reflected the great leader's honest nature. The young Washington reputedly cut down his father's cherry tree and, when asked if this was so, replied: "I cannot tell a lie. I did it."

Early banknote bearing the image of George Washington, 1800

Handkerchief with a map of Washington, D.C.

THE NATION'S CAPITAL

In 1791, George Washington helped select a site on the Potomac River to be the nation's new capital. In his honor, the city was named Washington. As president, Washington played a major role in planning the design of the new federal city, which formed the District of Columbia.

George Washington

1ST PRESIDENT
1789–1797

BORN
February 22, 1732
Westmoreland County, Virginia

INAUGURATED AS PRESIDENT
First term: April 30, 1789
Second term: March 4, 1793

AGE AT INAUGURATION
57

PARTY
Federalist

FIRST LADY
Martha Dandridge Custis

CHILDREN ADOPTED BY MARRIAGE
John Parke Custis
Martha Parke Custis

DIED
December 14, 1799
Mount Vernon, Virginia

KEY EVENTS OF PRESIDENCY

1789 Washington appoints Thomas Jefferson as secretary of state and Alexander Hamilton as secretary of the treasury; John Adams is vice president.

1791 A national bank is established; the site for the nation's new capital, Washington, D.C., is selected; the first ten amendments of the Constitution are ratified.

1792 Congress establishes a national mint.

1793 Washington issues the Proclamation of Neutrality in an attempt to avoid conflict with Great Britain and France, who are at war.

1794 Washington signs the unpopular Jay Treaty with Great Britain allowing U.S. ships to be inspected at sea in return for the removal of British troops from the Northwest Territory; Washington puts down the Whiskey Rebellion.

John Adams

JOHN ADAMS WAS NOT A POPULAR hero like George Washington (p. 4). He could be pompous and stubborn and he made many political enemies. Yet he was one of the great Founding Fathers of the United States. Adams helped draft the Declaration of Independence and was one of its most enthusiastic supporters. He also served as an eminent diplomat in Europe, where he negotiated the treaty that ended the Revolution in 1783. He felt overlooked as George Washington's vice president, claiming the role was "the most insignificant office that ever the invention of man contrived." But his loyalty was rewarded. In 1797 Adams became the next president. Foreign affairs dominated his term of office, especially the war between Great Britain and France. To his credit, Adams managed to keep the United States out of the conflict and officially at peace.

John Adams was short and stout with a proud personality.

Cookbook used in the Adams family, c.1780

HIS ROTUNDITY

John Adams was born in Braintree, Massachusetts, and studied law at Harvard University. He worked as a lawyer in Boston before becoming involved in the American independence movement. By his own admission, Adams was "puffy, vain, conceited," and as George Washington's vice president, he encouraged the Senate to bestow grand titles on the members of the new government. It was not long before Adams's detractors were referring to him as "His Rotundity."

Father of the Navy

When Adams became president, Great Britain and France were at war. Although the United States was neutral, the French attacked U.S. ships to prevent them from trading with Great Britain. War with France seemed imminent, so Adams established a naval department and ordered warships to be built. Although war was never officially declared, for two years, French and U.S. frigates engaged in battle at sea. In 1800, Adams negotiated an end to the hostilities.

ABIGAIL ADAMS

Before he married his wife, Abigail, John Adams sent her a list of her "Faults, Imperfections, (and) Defects." Yet her faults must have been few, because she proved herself more than capable of the role of politician's wife and First Lady. While her husband was away on government business, often for years at a time, Abigail was left to run their farm in Massachusetts and bring up their children. Under her wise handling, the family prospered, and among her children, she reared a future president, John Quincy Adams (p. 15). The Adams's marriage was a happy one and lasted more than 50 years.

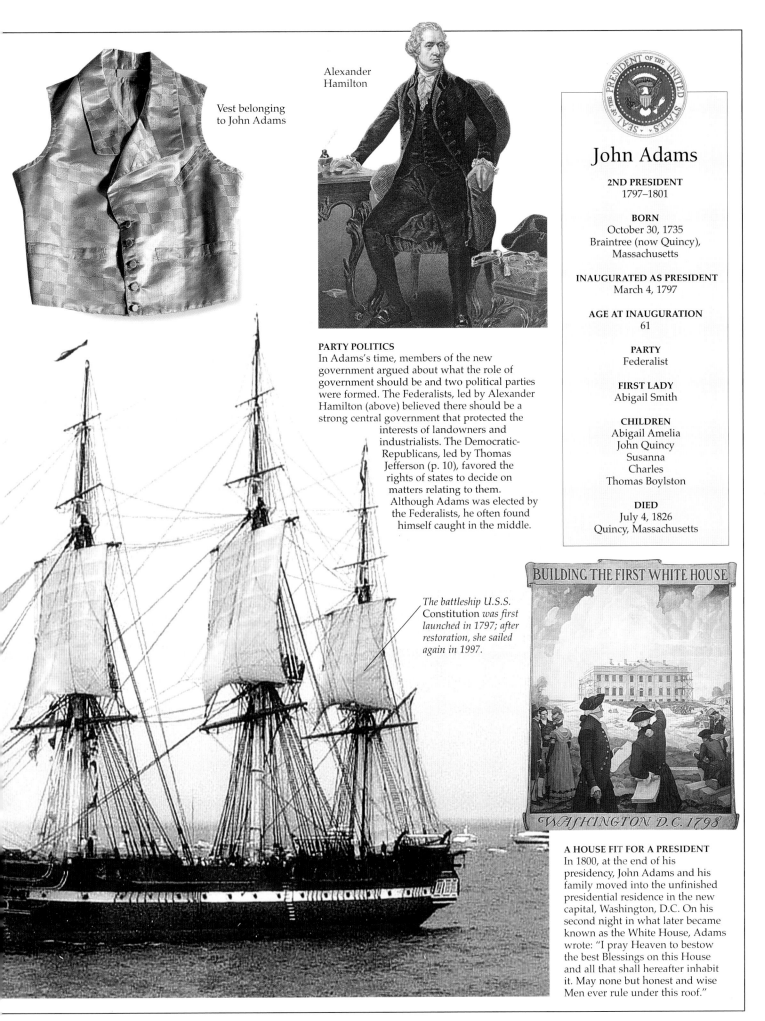

Vest belonging to John Adams

Alexander Hamilton

John Adams

2ND PRESIDENT
1797–1801

BORN
October 30, 1735
Braintree (now Quincy),
Massachusetts

INAUGURATED AS PRESIDENT
March 4, 1797

AGE AT INAUGURATION
61

PARTY
Federalist

FIRST LADY
Abigail Smith

CHILDREN
Abigail Amelia
John Quincy
Susanna
Charles
Thomas Boylston

DIED
July 4, 1826
Quincy, Massachusetts

PARTY POLITICS
In Adams's time, members of the new government argued about what the role of government should be and two political parties were formed. The Federalists, led by Alexander Hamilton (above) believed there should be a strong central government that protected the interests of landowners and industrialists. The Democratic-Republicans, led by Thomas Jefferson (p. 10), favored the rights of states to decide on matters relating to them. Although Adams was elected by the Federalists, he often found himself caught in the middle.

The battleship U.S.S. Constitution was first launched in 1797; after restoration, she sailed again in 1997.

BUILDING THE FIRST WHITE HOUSE

WASHINGTON D.C. 1798

A HOUSE FIT FOR A PRESIDENT
In 1800, at the end of his presidency, John Adams and his family moved into the unfinished presidential residence in the new capital, Washington, D.C. On his second night in what later became known as the White House, Adams wrote: "I pray Heaven to bestow the best Blessings on this House and all that shall hereafter inhabit it. May none but honest and wise Men ever rule under this roof."

Thomas Jefferson

Banner commemorating Jefferson's election, 1800

THOMAS JEFFERSON believed in a national government that had limited powers over the states and the people. Yet as president, he made bold decisions on behalf of his country. In 1803, he seized the opportunity to purchase the vast territory of Louisiana from France for 15 million dollars, even though the Constitution did not authorize him to do so. This doubled the size of the country and made westward expansion possible. Jefferson successfully kept the nation neutral during the Napoleonic Wars, although his ban on the shipping of American goods to warring Great Britain and France was neither popular nor effective. After eight years as president, Jefferson decided to step down because he believed that no leader should serve more than two terms.

JEFFERSON THE PATRIOT

A brilliant scholar and lawyer, Jefferson was elected to the Virginia House of Burgesses when he was 25. He became famous as a writer of eloquent political essays such as "A Summary View of the Rights of British America." At the start of the Revolutionary War (p. 4), Jefferson served in the Continental Congress, the body that acted on behalf of the colonies. He was also elected governor of Virginia and helped frame its revolutionary state constitution. In 1784, he went to Europe, joining John Adams (p. 8) and Benjamin Franklin to negotiate treaties with European powers. He returned in 1789 to take up his role as George Washington's (p. 4) secretary of state. In 1801, Jefferson himself became president.

Jefferson (right) writing the Declaration of Independence with John Adams (center) and Benjamin Franklin (left).

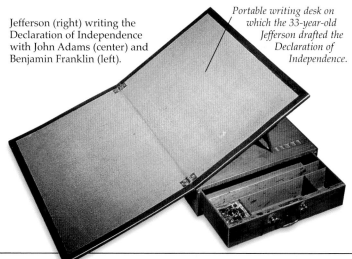

Portable writing desk on which the 33-year-old Jefferson drafted the Declaration of Independence.

The Declaration of Independence

At the Continental Congress in 1776, Thomas Jefferson was asked to write the Declaration of Independence. In this historic document, he stated the belief that all people had certain basic rights to life and liberty which no government could take away. The Declaration was addressed to the British king, George III, whom the Americans accused of stepping on their rights and freedoms. They argued that the American colonies should be "free and independent states."

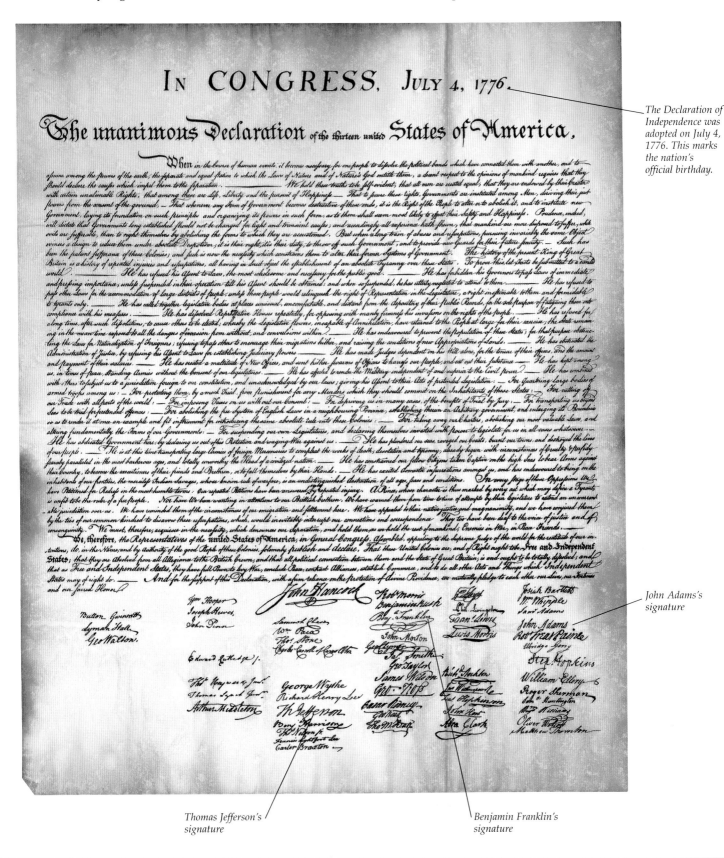

The Declaration of Independence was adopted on July 4, 1776. This marks the nation's official birthday.

John Adams's signature

Thomas Jefferson's signature

Benjamin Franklin's signature

11

Continued on next page

The great scholar

Thomas Jefferson was one of the most learned men in American history. He knew six different languages, studied music, law, science, and philosophy, and was a talented, self-taught architect. Jefferson's accomplishments reflected his varied interests. Not only did he write the Declaration of Independence, he championed religious freedom and public education, dispatched an expedition to discover the natural wonders of the continent, and pioneered neoclassical architecture in the United States.

MONTICELLO
One of Jefferson's many interests was architecture. Inspired by the work of the 16th-century Italian architect Andrea Palladio, he designed his own home on a hill above Charlottesville, Virginia. He named it Monticello, the Italian word for "little mountain." This elegant, 32-room house was surrounded by beautiful gardens. It was the embodiment of Jefferson's classical tastes and learning. He designed many special features for Monticello, such as a dumbwaiter in which food and wine could be raised from the cellar, swivel chairs, alcove beds, and an elaborate parquet floor for the parlor.

THE UNIVERSITY OF VIRGINIA
Jefferson believed strongly in education, in part so that American citizens could make informed decisions about public affairs. One of Jefferson's proudest achievements was his role in founding the University of Virginia. He recruited the teachers, planned the curriculum, and even designed the university buildings.

Colonnaded buildings designed by Jefferson

Sacagawea became a heroine in national folklore.

JEFFERSON AND RELIGION
Jefferson wrote his own interpretation of the New Testament in order to better understand what he thought were the true teachings of Jesus. He is also remembered for his ardent support of religious freedom. As a member of the Virginia legislature in the 1770s, he fought hard for a statute of religious freedom. He declared "eternal hostility against every form of tyranny over the mind of man." His statute was finally accepted in 1786.

The Jefferson Bible

Jefferson's gravestone

FINAL RESTING PLACE
Thomas Jefferson died on July 4, 1826, just a few hours before his fellow countryman John Adams (p. 8). He was laid to rest at Monticello. Jefferson left an epitaph to be inscribed on his gravestone, which read: "Here was buried Thomas Jefferson, Author of the Declaration of Independence, of the Statute of Virginia for Religious Freedom, and the Father of the University of Virginia." Jefferson chose not to mention that he had also been president of the United States.

THE LEWIS AND CLARK EXPEDITION

Jefferson was a keen amateur naturalist, and he was eager to find out about the American interior. In 1804, he sent an expedition, led by Meriwether Lewis and William Clark, to explore the newly acquired Louisiana Territory. Lewis and Clark were aided by a Shoshone girl named Sacagawea, who helped them communicate with the different Native American peoples they met. Over two years, the expedition members traveled as far as the Pacific Ocean. They kept detailed accounts of the plants, animals, and birds they saw, as well as mapped the natural features of the continent.

This is the compass carried by the explorers on the Lewis and Clark expedition.

Meriwether Lewis was appointed governor of the Louisiana Territory upon his return in 1806.

William Clark became superintendent of Indian affairs in the Louisiana Territory and later governor of the Missouri Territory.

Thomas Jefferson

3RD PRESIDENT
1801–1809

BORN
April 13, 1743
Albemarle County, Virginia

INAUGURATED AS PRESIDENT
First term: March 4, 1801
Second term: March 4, 1805

AGE AT INAUGURATION
57

PARTY
Democratic-Republican

WIFE
Martha Wayles Skelton
(died 1782)

CHILDREN
Martha
Maria
Lucy Elizabeth

DIED
July 4, 1826
Charlottesville, Virginia

KEY EVENTS OF PRESIDENCY

1801 Jefferson sends the navy to quell the Barbary pirates in the Mediterranean.

1803 In the Marbury v. Madison case, the Supreme Court declares an act of Congress to be unconstitutional for the first time; Jefferson makes the Louisiana Purchase.

1804 Jefferson is reelected as president; Jefferson's rival, Aaron Burr, kills Alexander Hamilton in a duel; the Lewis and Clark Expedition sets off.

1806 Aaron Burr tries to incite a rebellion in Louisiana.

1807 Burr is arrested and tried for treason, but is acquitted; the U.S. frigate *Chesapeake* is fired upon and boarded by the British warship *Leopard*—Jefferson sticks to his policy of neutrality and avoids a declaration of war; Jefferson signs the Embargo Act banning the export of U.S. goods to Europe in retaliation for the *Chesapeake* incident.

1808 Jefferson prohibits the import of slaves from Africa.

James Madison

James Madison was a great political thinker. In 1787, he was a leader in framing the Constitution of the United States and was nicknamed the "Father of the Constitution." One of the delegates to the Constitutional Convention (p. 5) wrote about Madison: "Every person seems to acknowledge his greatness. In the management of every question he took the lead." After serving as Thomas Jefferson's (p. 10) secretary of state for eight years, Madison became president in 1809. During his administration, the United States became involved in the War of 1812 with Great Britain. The war went badly for the United States and people referred to it bitterly as "Mr. Madison's War." But Madison's reputation was rescued, in part, when U.S. troops under General Andrew Jackson (p. 16) won a brilliant victory at the Battle of New Orleans in 1815.

THE BILL OF RIGHTS
Although he helped create the Constitution, Madison felt that it did not do enough to protect the rights of individual citizens. In the 1780s, he led the fight to have safeguards built into the Constitution. These took the form of the first ten amendments, which became known as the Bill of Rights. Adopted in 1791, it guaranteed freedom of speech, religion, and assembly, and the right to trial by jury.

In stature, James Madison was the nation's smallest president. He was scarcely five feet six inches tall and weighed only about 100 pounds.

MR. MADISON'S WAR
In June, 1812, a powerful group of politicians known as the War Hawks persuaded the president to declare war on Great Britain. There were strong reasons for the war—continued British harassment of U.S. ships and the kidnapping of American sailors— but Madison was reluctant all the same. His country was ill-prepared to fight, and the war did, indeed, go badly for the young nation.

WASHINGTON IN FLAMES
The year 1814 was a bleak time for President Madison. In August, British forces invaded and burned the nation's capital, Washington, D.C. A peace treaty was signed later that year, but neither the United States nor Great Britain could be said to have won the war.

The British army lost three generals at the Battle of New Orleans in 1815.

A PLUCKY FIRST LADY
Dolley Madison's lavish White House parties became famous. She was a popular First Lady who also knew how to keep her head in a crisis. When the British invaded the city of Washington, Dolley was told to flee the White House. In the president's absence, she calmly packed up her husband's papers, the national seal, and a portrait of George Washington, and sent them on ahead before leaving herself. Shortly after, British troops set fire to the White House.

James Monroe

James Monroe was the last of the Revolutionary Patriots to become president. He had studied law under Thomas Jefferson, helped negotiate the Louisiana Purchase from France, and served as secretary of state and secretary of war under Madison. Monroe's presidency was known as the "Era of Good Feelings" because the nation was politically tranquil and at peace. Yet not everything was ideal. There was a depression in 1819, and the next year, the Missouri Compromise ignited angry debates about the extension of slavery in the new states and territories. Monroe is best remembered, though, for his famous foreign policy doctrine.

Serious by nature, Monroe proved to be a popular president.

Monroe's own handwritten draft of the Monroe Doctrine

THE MONROE DOCTRINE
In December, 1823, President Monroe announced his new foreign policy. He declared that the United States would not look kindly on European nations that tried to interfere in North and South American affairs. Furthermore, he warned against any new attempts to establish colonies in the Americas by European powers. This bold policy soon became known as the Monroe Doctrine.

John Quincy Adams

John Quincy Adams was the son of former president John Adams (p. 8). Like his father, John Quincy Adams had a sober personality. He was more interested in scholarly pursuits than in card playing and dancing. His good education and talent for learning languages contributed to his great success as a diplomat. Yet as president, Adams was not as successful. He found that the people were not interested in his advanced ideas for spending their taxes on internal improvements—roads and canals—and scientific explorations. Adams was not reelected.

Portrait of John Quincy Adams painted in 1844

DEATH IN THE HOUSE
John Quincy Adams did not retire from public office when he lost the election of 1828. Instead, he embarked on a long and distinguished career in the House of Representatives, where he was a vigorous opponent of slavery. In 1848, at the age of 80, Adams suffered a stroke while seated in the House. He was carried to the Speaker's Room, where he died two days later. His last words were: "Thank the officers of the House. This is the last of earth. I am content."

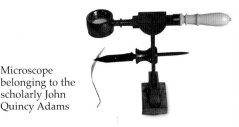

Microscope belonging to the scholarly John Quincy Adams

James Madison

4TH PRESIDENT
1809–1817
BORN
March 16, 1751, Port Conway, Virginia
DIED
June 28, 1836, Montpelier, Virginia

James Monroe

5TH PRESIDENT
1817–1825
BORN
April 28, 1758, Westmoreland County, Virginia
DIED
July 4, 1831, New York City, New York

John Quincy Adams

6TH PRESIDENT
1825–1829
BORN
July 11, 1767, Quincy, Massachusetts
DIED
February 23, 1848, Washington, D.C.

Andrew Jackson

Woman's decorative comb bearing Jackson's image

Snuff box with Jackson depicted as a military hero, 1828

Pot metal statuette of General Andrew Jackson

ANDREW JACKSON WAS the first president to be born in a log cabin, and he brought a feisty, frontier spirit to the White House. He believed that as president it was his job to represent the interests of ordinary American citizens. He fought constantly with Congress and used his powers to veto any legislation that he thought favored the wealthy elite. This policy became known as "Jacksonian democracy." Jackson's popularity with the voters soared and he was easily reelected to a second term.

INAUGURATION DAY ANTICS
Wealthy politicians in Congress were worried when Andrew Jackson was elected president. They thought it would be the beginning of mob rule. Events on Jackson's inauguration day seemed to confirm their fears. Rowdy supporters crowded into the White House to celebrate Jackson's victory and he was forced to flee.

Andrew Jackson

7TH PRESIDENT
1829–1837

BORN
March 15, 1767
The Waxhaws, South Carolina

INAUGURATED AS PRESIDENT
First term: March 4, 1829
Second term: March 4, 1833

AGE AT INAUGURATION
61

PARTY
Democratic

WIFE
Rachel Donelson Robards
(died 1828)

WARD
Andrew Jackson, Jr.

DIED
June 8, 1845
Nashville, Tennessee

A BATTLEFIELD HERO FOR PRESIDENT
Andrew Jackson was born in poverty. His Irish father died before he was born and the young Jackson lost his mother when he was aged 15, leaving him to make his way in the world alone. Despite receiving little education, Jackson succeeded in becoming both a prosperous planter and a judge in Tennessee. He also enjoyed a legendary military career. He earned himself the nickname "Hero of New Orleans" for defeating the British army in the War of 1812 (p. 14). Jackson was the second battlefield hero to become president after George Washington (p. 4).

Jackson was a tall, commanding man and cut a dashing figure.

Jackson is dressed in the blue general's coat that he may have worn at the Battle of New Orleans.

All 183 of the Texan rebels were killed.

KING ANDREW

Many politicians thought President Jackson abused his position of power in the name of the people. In their opinion, Jackson too often vetoed, or rejected, legislation as he saw fit, rather than giving in to the will of Congress. His enemies named him "King Andrew," implying that he behaved more like a king than an elected president. But Jackson set new precedents and significantly strengthened the role of the president.

Cartoon portrays Jackson as a king with a scepter in one hand and a document declaring his power of veto in the other.

THE ALAMO

When Jackson became president, Texas belonged to Mexico, although Jackson was keen for Texas to join the Union. The president's wish was in part fulfilled by a series of events in 1835 and 1836. When the Mexican government outlawed slavery in Texas, the white settlers there were furious. In an act of rebellion, a group of them captured the town of San Antonio, but the angry Mexicans sent in the army. The siege of the Alamo began. After 13 days, the large Mexican force attacked and the rebels were killed. But the Texans did not give up. Six weeks later, they defeated the Mexicans at San Jacinto and won their independence. The territory was now free to join the Union.

Dueling pistols c.1800

DARING DUELS

By nature, Andrew Jackson was temperamental and sensitive to insults. He once shot and killed a man in a duel over an unkind remark about his wife, Rachel.

Gold epaulettes

FORCING THE INDIANS WEST

As a frontier general, Jackson had fought in the war with the Creek Indians. The Creeks called him "Sharp Knife," a name Jackson lived up to. During his first term as president, he signed the Indian Removal Act (1830). This allowed the government to forcibly remove Native Americans from their eastern homelands to the frontier, west of the Mississippi River.

Dance wand from the Cherokee tribe, whose land in Georgia was confiscated by Jackson's government

This humorous 1834 biography of Jackson satirizes the president and makes fun of his heroic image. It purports to be written by a Major Jack Downing, but was really the work of humorist Seba Smith of New England.

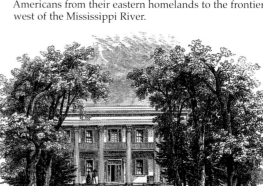

THE HERMITAGE

Jackson became a prosperous planter, and in later life he lived in a mansion called the Hermitage near Nashville, Tennessee. Jackson and his wife Rachel are buried in the garden near the house.

Martin Van Buren

Martin Van Buren inspired many nicknames, most of which alluded to his political cunning. He was called the "Little Magician" and compared to a fox. Van Buren had been Andrew Jackson's (p. 16) trusted vice president. Jackson chose his friend to be the next president, and the voters supported Jackson's choice. Unfortunately, a severe economic depression followed Van Buren to the White House. When he could not find a solution, short of magic, to bring back prosperity, he was voted out of office.

An early photograph, or daguerrotype, of Van Buren in later years

THE CHAMPAGNE-DRINKING PRESIDENT
President Van Buren had expensive tastes for which he was sometimes criticized. During the election campaign of 1840 against William Henry Harrison, Van Buren was portrayed as an irresponsible dandy who dressed himself in finery while the country was in the midst of economic depression.

President Van Buren smiles when he sips champagne…

…and frowns when he tastes common cider!

Campaign item from the 1840 election

THE TRAIL OF TEARS
Van Buren continued Andrew Jackson's Indian removal policies. Between 1838 and 1839, 15,000 Cherokee were escorted by federal troops from their Georgia homeland to reservations in the West. They were forced to march without rest, and many of their number died along the way. Their journey became known as the "Trail of Tears."

About 4,000 Cherokee died on the 116-day journey to what is now Oklahoma.

The Cherokee were forced to travel in the bitter cold of autumn and winter with inadequate supplies of food.

William Henry Harrison

William Henry Harrison was born at Berkeley, a colonial plantation on the James River in southern Virginia. His father had signed the Declaration of Independence and his grandson, Benjamin Harrison (p. 33), would later become president. Harrison was a military hero. In 1811, he defeated the Indian chief Tecumseh and his Shawnee warriors at the Battle of Tippecanoe in the Indiana Territory. Harrison, however, is remembered largely for quite another reason. A month after he was inaugurated, he died of pneumonia, serving the shortest term of any president.

THE LOG CABIN CAMPAIGN
In the presidential election of 1840, Harrison's supporters led people to believe their candidate had grown up poor in a log cabin, instead of in an elegant mansion. This was the famous "log cabin and hard cider campaign," popular symbols used to attract the votes of the common man.

A PRESIDENT'S DEATHBED
Sixty-eight-year-old Harrison caught cold, which developed into pneumonia, after delivering the longest inaugural address ever on a bitterly cold March day. Doctors fought hard to save the president, but he died on April 4, exactly one month to the day after his inauguration.

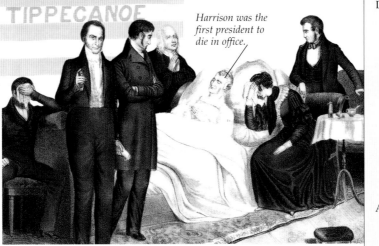

Harrison was the first president to die in office.

Martin Van Buren

8TH PRESIDENT
1837–1841
BORN
December 5, 1782, Kinderhook, New York
DIED
July 24, 1862, Kinderhook, New York

William Henry Harrison

9TH PRESIDENT
1841
BORN
February 9, 1773, Berkeley, Virginia
DIED
April 4, 1841, Washington, D.C.

John Tyler

10TH PRESIDENT
1841–1845
BORN
March 29, 1790, Charles City County, Virginia
DIED
January 18, 1862, Richmond, Virginia

John Tyler

Upon Harrison's death, John Tyler became the first vice president to be made president of the United States. Tyler belonged to the Whig Party. Yet he did not support many of the things the Whigs believed in, such as a national bank, federally funded roads and canals, and high tariffs to protect northern industries. Worse still, Tyler supported slavery, which many Whigs denounced. He became an outcast in his own party. Many of Tyler's critics challenged his right to call himself president, because he had not been elected. They referred to him as "Acting President Tyler" and nicknamed him "His Accidency." Tyler proudly refused to open any mail addressed to the "Acting President."

A TRUE PRESIDENT
Tyler set an important precedent for future vice presidents who became president, because he steadfastly exercised all of the powers and privileges of the presidency.

THE NEW MRS. TYLER
John Tyler was the first president to be married while in office. In 1844, he married the young and vivacious Julia Gardiner, who was 30 years his junior.

James K. Polk

Polk's eyeglasses

"WHO IS JAMES K. POLK?" exclaimed a rival candidate in the election of 1844. Polk, a Democrat, was a former speaker of the House of Representatives and a governor of Tennessee. Few people, however, saw him as a presidential candidate. Once in the White House, though, Polk proved to be a diligent worker. He believed that the United States should fulfill its "manifest destiny" of expanding westward to the Pacific Ocean. In 1846, a border dispute in the new state of Texas triggered a war with Mexico. At the Treaty of Guadalupe Hidalgo (1848) that followed, the victorious Americans acquired California and New Mexico. In the Pacific Northwest, Polk settled a long dispute with Great Britain over the northern boundary of the Oregon Territory at the Forty-ninth Parallel. When he left office, the country spanned two oceans.

James K. Polk

11TH PRESIDENT
1845–1849

BORN
November 2, 1795
Mecklenburg County,
North Carolina

INAUGURATED AS PRESIDENT
March 4, 1845

AGE AT INAUGURATION
49

PARTY
Democratic

FIRST LADY
Sarah Childress

CHILDREN
None

DIED
June 15, 1849
Nashville,
Tennessee

THE MEXICAN WAR
President Polk first tried to buy the southwestern territories he desired from the Mexicans. When they turned down his offer, Polk instigated the Mexican War. The brilliant leadership of General Zachary Taylor and the U.S. Army's superior weaponry led to the defeat of the Mexican forces in 1848, allowing Polk to fulfill his territorial aims.

1,000 Colt revolvers were issued to U.S. soldiers in the Mexican War.

General Taylor's faithful horse, Whitey, became almost as famous as his master during the Mexican War.

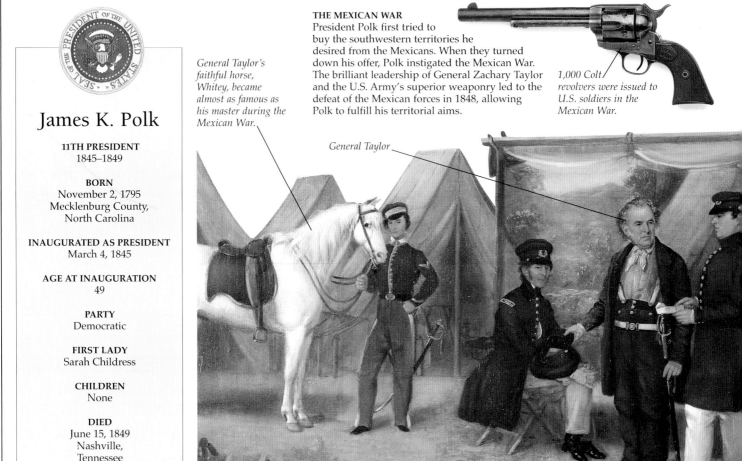

General Taylor

Zachary Taylor

Nicknamed "Old Rough and Ready," Zachary Taylor was a professional soldier with no political experience. The hero of the Mexican War, he won the election of 1848 mainly because of his popularity. When he took office, the extension of slavery in the new southwestern territories was the pressing issue of the day. Taylor did not want the new territories to become slave states. He wanted to keep the peace between the North, where slavery was regarded as an evil, and the South, which relied upon slave labor. Taylor threatened to veto the Compromise of 1850—a series of measures designed to resolve the issue—because he thought that it favored the slave states. Fatefully, he died unexpectedly that year.

Although he looks smart in this official portrait, Taylor was often dressed in rumpled clothes and was said to look more like a farmer than a man destined for the White House.

California gold-miners were called Fortyniners.

CALIFORNIA GOLD RUSH
When gold was discovered in California in 1848, it made the slavery question all the more pressing. In 1849, thousands of prospectors poured into the territory hoping to make their fortunes. Taylor wanted to see California enter the United States as a free (nonslave) state.

Zachary Taylor

12TH PRESIDENT
1849–1850

BORN
November 24, 1784
Montebello, Virginia

INAUGURATED AS PRESIDENT
March 5, 1849

AGE AT INAUGURATION
64

PARTY
Whig

FIRST LADY
Margaret Mackall Smith

CHILDREN
Ann Mackall
Sarah Knox
Octavia Pannill
Margaret Smith
Mary Elizabeth
Richard

DIED
July 9, 1850
Washington, D.C.

BUENA VISTA VETERAN
Zachary Taylor was a veteran of the War of 1812, and of two Indian wars, the Black Hawk War in Illinois in 1832 and the Seminole War in Florida in 1836–37. He became a hero, though, for his splendid victories in the Mexican War, most notably at the Battle of Buena Vista in 1847. There, he defeated the superior forces of General Santa Anna, losing only 700 men to the Mexicans' 1,500. Taylor's military successes earned him enormous national acclaim and helped him win the presidency in 1848. His popularity was so enduring that when he died in 1850 from an intestinal disorder, thousands of mourners lined the route of his funeral procession.

Taylor with members of his staff at his military encampment during the Mexican War

Millard Fillmore

Slave collar

Portrait of Fillmore c.1840

Millard Fillmore grew up poor on a farm in New York state. He had little formal education, but was tutored by a young schoolteacher, Abigail Powers, whom he later married. In 1849, Fillmore became Zachary Taylor's (p. 21) vice president, and then president himself after Taylor's sudden death. Unlike Taylor, Fillmore favored the Compromise of 1850 (p. 21), which temporarily prevented the Union from breaking up. By signing the Fugitive Slave Act, though, Fillmore lost the support of the northerners in his Whig party and was not reelected.

PERRY'S MISSION TO JAPAN
In 1853, Fillmore sent Commodore Matthew Perry on a mission to Japan. Perry had orders to establish trade links with the Japanese, who had refused to trade with other countries for 200 years. Intimidated by U.S. naval power, the Japanese emperor agreed to open his ports to U.S. shipping.

135,000 SETS. 270,000 VOLUMES SOLD.

UNCLE TOM'S CABIN

FOR SALE HERE.

The Greatest Book of the Age.

THE FUGITIVE SLAVE ACT
The most controversial part of the Compromise of 1850 was the Fugitive Slave Act. It promised federal support for returning runaway slaves to their owners, allowing escaped slaves to be hunted down in the North. While southern slaveholders approved, northern abolitionists were outraged.

UNCLE TOM'S CABIN
Harriet Beecher Stowe was an abolitionist (someone who wanted to abolish slavery) from the North. She was horrified by the passing of the Fugitive Slave Act. In 1852, she published a novel called *Uncle Tom's Cabin* that highlighted the wrongs of slavery. Her book sold thousands of copies and helped strengthen antislavery sentiment throughout the country.

Franklin Pierce

Millard Fillmore

13TH PRESIDENT
1850–1853
BORN
January 7, 1800, Cayuga County, New York
DIED
March 8, 1874, Buffalo, New York

Franklin Pierce

14TH PRESIDENT
1853–1857
BORN
November 23, 1804, Hilsboro, New Hampshire
DIED
October 8, 1869, Concord, New Hampshire

James Buchanan

15TH PRESIDENT
1857–1861
BORN
April 23, 1791, Cove Gap, Pennsylvania
DIED
June 1, 1868, Lancaster, Pennsylvania

Just weeks before Franklin Pierce became president, his eleven-year-old son, Benjamin, was killed in a train wreck. This sad event cast a shadow over his presidency. Once in office, Pierce, a New England lawyer, tried his best to keep the peace between the North and the South. Yet he made a fateful decision in supporting the controversial Kansas-Nebraska Act (1854). This act left settlers to decide on the critical question of whether or not to allow slavery in their territories. It provoked vicious fighting in what became known as "Bleeding Kansas." Indeed, the entire country stepped closer toward fighting a civil war.

Daguerrotype of Pierce c.1852; his nickname was "Handsome Frank."

ATTACK IN THE SENATE
The Kansas-Nebraska Act aroused strong emotions on all sides. During the passage of the act, southern representative Preston Brooks attacked his antislavery colleague, Senator Charles Sumner. Sumner collapsed and did not fully recover for several years.

"Border Ruffians" from Missouri prowled through Kansas looking for abolitionists.

BLEEDING KANSAS
After the Kansas-Nebraska Act was passed, northern abolitionists flooded into Kansas hoping to vote in a Free-Soil (antislave) party. But Kansas bordered on Missouri, which was a slaveholding state. In 1855, thousands of Missourians crossed into Kansas to vote against the abolitionists. When a proslavery government was elected, a bloody border war broke out between the two opposing sides.

James Buchanan

The presidency of James Buchanan was doomed from the start. For ten years the slavery debate had troubled the occupants of the White House, and Buchanan was no exception. A former lawyer from the North, he argued that slavery was legal under the constitution and urged for compromise on the issue. But the abolitionist movement was growing in strength. In both the North and the South, trust and reason were rapidly giving way to fear and anger. Buchanan became a pathetic spectator as events in the country spun out of control. By the time he left office, civil war was inevitable.

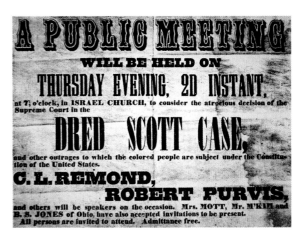

Buchanan, a courtly mannered bachelor, was tall and dignified. He served with merit in public life for 40 years.

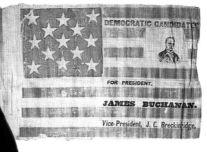

Campaign flag for Democratic candidate James Buchanan

THE DRED SCOTT DECISION
In 1857, the Supreme Court made a historic ruling in a case brought by a slave, Dred Scott. Scott was suing his owner for his freedom on the basis that he had lived in a free state and this made him free. The Court ruled that Scott was not a citizen and therefore could not file a lawsuit. This decision dealt a blow to the abolitionist cause.

JOHN BROWN'S RAID
John Brown was a radical abolitionist who, in 1859, attempted to start a slave rebellion. His aim was to capture the federal arsenal at Harper's Ferry, Virginia, and establish a base from which he could mount raids against slave owners. His plan failed, and Brown was captured and hanged. Yet the legend of John Brown lived on—in poetry and song— and struck fear into the hearts of many southerners.

Free-Soil activists in Kansas armed with a cannon

THE FREE-SOIL CAUSE
Buchanan urged Congress to accept Kansas as a slave state. In 1858, though, the proslavery constitution in Kansas was voted out. Members of the Free-Soil Party joined the newly formed Republican Party, which supported their abolitionist ideas. The Bleeding Kansas issue provided them with a strong antislavery platform in the 1860 election. That year, the Republican candidate, Abraham Lincoln (p. 24), was elected president. Kansas was finally admitted to the Union as a free state in 1861.

FREDERICK DOUGLASS
A former slave, Frederick Douglass was the foremost black abolitionist of his time. He was a brilliant orator and ran his own antislavery newspaper, the *North Star*. After John Brown's raid, President Buchanan sent federal agents to arrest Douglass. Douglass fled the country, but returned soon after to continue his fight.

Abraham Lincoln

BORN IN 1809, ABRAHAM LINCOLN GREW UP in humble surroundings on the frontier. He became a lawyer and a politician, and was a strong believer in liberty for all Americans. He especially deplored slavery and spoke out firmly against the evils of its expansion. In 1860, Lincoln was elected president. The southern states viewed him as a threat to their slave culture. They left the Union to form the Confederate States of America. Lincoln faced a country divided against itself and on the brink of civil war. It became his sole purpose to bind the nation together again, an enormous task that no president, before or since, has had to undertake.

MARY TODD LINCOLN
Lincoln's wife Mary found her role as First Lady difficult, and she was unpopular in Washington. Both the Civil War (she was a southerner) and the death of her son Willie in 1862 had a harmful effect on her fragile mental health.

Lincoln's clothes often appeared ill-fitting, and his homely appearance sometimes provoked criticism.

OLD ABE,
ICH   MEIN.
PRINCE OF RAILS.

This wooden ax symbolized Lincoln's rail-splitting days and was carried in campaign parades.

HONEST ABE
In the presidential campaign of 1860, Lincoln's Republican supporters emphasized his humble origins. They wanted to present Lincoln as a good man who had worked his way to the top through honest labor. Lincoln was nicknamed "Prince of Rails" in reference to one of his early jobs as a rail-splitter. Lincoln also worked as a ferryboat captain, a store clerk, a surveyor, and a postmaster before becoming a lawyer in Springfield, Illinois.

AN UNLIKELY LEADER
According to a close friend, Abraham Lincoln was driven by "a little engine that knew no rest." An ambitious young man, he trained himself to be a lawyer and was later elected to the state legislature of Illinois. He was elected to Congress, and became famous for his antislavery opinions. The Republican party named Lincoln its presidential candidate in 1860 and he was elected with a mere 40 percent of the votes. Although he became one of the greatest presidents in American history, Lincoln did not cut a dashing figure. At six feet, four inches, he often appeared awkward and spoke with a "frontier" accent in a high, reedy voice.

LINCOLN AND SLAVERY

In the years before the Civil War, the southern states relied upon slave labor to produce the rice, cotton, and sugarcane on which their economy depended. Although Abraham Lincoln regarded slavery as unjust, he did not believe in forcing the southern states to abolish it. But he did want to prevent new territories in the West from becoming slave states. Many people were drawn to Lincoln's moderate approach. When he was elected president in 1860, many southerners believed this signaled the end of slavery and their accustomed way of life.

Many slaves escaped to the free states in the North via the Underground Railroad, a system of safe houses operated by abolitionists.

A group of runaway slaves

Abraham Lincoln

16TH PRESIDENT
1861–1865

BORN
February 12, 1809
Hardin County, Kentucky

INAUGURATED AS PRESIDENT
First term: March 4, 1861
Second term: March 4, 1865

AGE AT INAUGURATION
52

PARTY
Republican

FIRST LADY
Mary Todd

CHILDREN
Robert Todd
Edward Baker
William Wallace
Thomas (Tad)

DIED
April 15, 1865
Washington, D.C.

KEY EVENTS OF PRESIDENCY

1861 Eleven southern states secede from the Union to create the Confederate States of America; Jefferson Davis is elected president of the Confederacy; Civil War breaks out when Confederates fire on Fort Sumter; the Union army is defeated at the first battle at Bull Run.

1862 The Confederates are stopped at Antietam; the Union army is defeated at Fredericksburg.

1863 Lincoln issues his Emancipation Proclamation, freeing all slaves in areas of rebellion; the Confederates are defeated at Gettysburg; Grant wins at Vicksburg.

1864 Grant is made commander of the Union forces; Lincoln is reelected unanimously; Union forces march through Georgia; the Confederates abandon Atlanta.

1865 The Union army captures Richmond; General Lee surrenders at Appomattox; Lincoln is assassinated.

THE UNION IS DISSOLVED!

Passed unanimously at 1.15 o'clock, P. M., December 20th, 1860.

AN ORDINANCE.

To dissolve the Union between the State of South Carolina and other States united with her under the compact entitled "The Constitution of the United States of America."

CHARLESTON MERCURY EXTRA

The Union collapses

Rather than accept Abraham Lincoln as their president, most southern states chose to secede, or separate, from the Union in 1861. Lincoln did not believe the southern states had a constitutional right to secede. He had sworn to uphold the laws of the land, and he was determined to reunite the country, even if it meant fighting a civil war.

South Carolina was the first state to secede. This extra from the Charleston Mercury newspaper announces that decision.

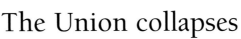
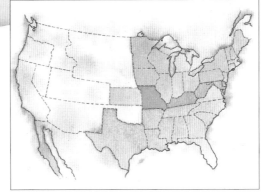

JEFFERSON DAVIS

In February, 1861, delegates from the Confederate states met in Montgomery, Alabama, to elect a president. They chose Jefferson Davis of Mississippi. Davis had entered Congress in 1845 and had been a commander in the Mexican War (p. 20). He served in the Senate and was secretary of war under President Pierce (p. 22). Davis was a slave owner and supported the continuation of slavery.

A NATION DIVIDED

In early 1861, South Carolina, Georgia, Florida, Alabama, Mississippi, and Louisiana formed a new nation, the Confederate States of America. One week after Abraham Lincoln was inaugurated, the Confederate States adopted a constitution recognizing their rights as separate states and protecting slavery. In all, 11 states (shown in purple) broke away from the Union (green), while five border states (orange) stayed in the Union, although some of their citizens supported the Confederacy.

Continued on next page

The Civil War

On April 12, 1861, Confederates fired on Fort Sumter, a Union stronghold in Charleston harbor, South Carolina. After 34 hours of heavy bombardment, the soldiers of the Union garrison were forced to evacuate by steamer. The attack was a near bloodless beginning to the bloodiest conflict in American history. The vicious fighting of the Civil War was to last four agonizing years. Lincoln was deeply pained by the bloodshed and often could be seen pacing the streets of Washington, D.C., late at night. But he never lost faith in his cause and under his firm leadership the Union eventually prevailed.

"Stars and Bars" Confederate flag

Accurate guns with rifled, or grooved, barrels were used in war for the first time, resulting in heavy casualties.

Confederate uniform cap, called a kepi

Abraham Lincoln and General George B. McClellan at the battlefield of Antietam, Maryland, September, 1862

This bullet-torn Confederate jacket was found on the battlefield of Seven Pines, Virginia.

ON THE BATTLEFIELD

The Civil War was one of America's bitterest conflicts. Soldiers on both sides fought fiercely for their causes. Because of the introduction of effective new weapons, losses were heavy. At the Battle of Gettysburg alone (1863), over 50,000 men were lost. In all, some 600,000 soldiers—two percent of the population—died in the war.

Union uniform kepi

Engraving portraying Lincoln as the liberator of the slaves

GRANT AND HIS GENERALS

It fell to Lincoln to raise an army and find good generals to lead it to victory. This became a slow, trial-by-error process, for which Lincoln received much criticism. He appointed and dismissed several generals. Meanwhile, the Confederates, under Robert E. Lee, were winning key battles. Finally, Lincoln gave command of the Union forces to Ulysses S. Grant (p. 29) and the North began to win the war.

General Grant

FREEING THE SLAVES

With the Emancipation Proclamation, signed in 1863, Lincoln freed slaves in the Confederate states. Slaves were considered Confederate property, and as commander in chief of the Union forces, Lincoln was entitled to order the seizure of enemy property. He had no constitutional right, however, to order the freeing of slaves in the North. Nevertheless, African Americans throughout the country rejoiced.

THE GETTYSBURG ADDRESS

In November, 1863, Lincoln arrived at Gettysburg, Pennsylvania, to dedicate a new Union cemetery. It was the site of the deadliest battle of the Civil War. There, in his most famous speech, Lincoln pledged "that these dead shall not have died in vain—that this nation, under God, shall have a new birth of freedom—and that government of the people, by the people, for the people, shall not perish from the earth."

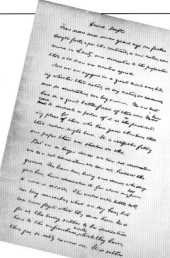

Copy of Lincoln's own draft of the Gettysburg Address

Photograph of Lincoln taken in 1865

The legendary Southern general, Robert E. Lee

Victorious Northern general Ulysses S. Grant

Lee and Grant shake hands

LEE SURRENDERS

On April 9, 1865, Confederate general Robert E. Lee surrendered to the Union commander Ulysses S. Grant at Appomattox Court House, Virginia. The Union's relentless campaign, coupled with the South's poor resources and desertions, had defeated the Confederacy. Lincoln's greatest wish at this time was to secure "a just and lasting peace," with "malice toward none, with charity for all."

LINCOLN IS ASSASSINATED

On April 14, 1865, five days after Lee's army surrendered, President Lincoln attended a performance of *Our American Cousin* at Ford's Theater, Washington, D.C. During the third act, a Confederate sympathizer, John Wilkes Booth, snuck into Lincoln's box and shot the president in the back of the head. Lincoln was carried to a nearby boardinghouse, where he died just after seven the following morning.

Sheet music of Lincoln's funeral march

THE NATION MOURNS

The assassination of Abraham Lincoln stunned and saddened the nation. Northerners wept for their lost leader. Tens of thousands of mourners viewed Lincoln's body as it lay in state and was then transported back to his home state. He was finally laid to rest on May 4, 1865, at Oak Ridge Cemetery in Springfield, Illinois. The nation had lost a great leader at the time when he was still badly needed. Lincoln had not believed in punishing the South for the war. With him gone, those bent on revenge were able to gain influence.

Memorial fan depicting Lincoln's assassination

Andrew Johnson

AT THE START OF the Civil War (p. 26), Andrew Johnson, a Democrat from Tennessee, was the only United States senator from the South to remain loyal to the Union. For his steadfastness, Johnson was nominated vice president in 1864. In April, 1865, after Lincoln (p. 24) was assassinated, Johnson became president. He tried to enact Lincoln's policy of leniency toward the defeated southern states. But a group of congressmen called the Radical Republicans resented giving too much power back to the former Confederates. When Johnson refused to yield to their demands, the Radicals in Congress impeached him.

Vest made by Johnson

THE TENNESSEE TAILOR
Johnson was nicknamed the "Tennessee Tailor" because he began his working life as a tailor's apprentice. He received no formal schooling and his wife, Eliza, taught him how to read and write. By the age of 33, Johnson was elected to Congress.

Andrew Johnson

17TH PRESIDENT
1865–1869

BORN
December 29, 1808
Raleigh, North Carolina

INAUGURATED AS PRESIDENT
April 15, 1865

AGE AT INAUGURATION
56

PARTY
Democratic

FIRST LADY
Eliza McCardle

CHILDREN
Martha
Charles
Mary
Robert
Andrew

DIED
July 31, 1875
Carter County, Tennessee

JOHNSON IN CARICATURE
Although the Thirteenth Amendment (1865) freed all slaves, many southern states still tried to deny African Americans the rights of citizenship. This anti-Johnson cartoon portrays the president as Iago, an evil character from Shakespeare's play *Othello*. He is whispering false promises to Othello, who is shown here as a wounded African American war veteran. The satire is clear: Johnson is betraying the free blacks who helped win the Civil War and the thousands of former slaves in the South.

Johnson portrayed as the traitor, Iago

Radical Republican political sketch shows former slaves being massacred in the South

THE PRESIDENT IS IMPEACHED
In 1868, Andrew Johnson became the first president in history to be impeached, or put on trial, by the Senate. There were no constitutional grounds for prosecuting Johnson, just political disagreements over his postwar Reconstruction policies. Although he was spared removal from office by one vote, his presidency was all but over.

Members of the House of Representatives who prosecuted Johnson

Ticket for the impeachment trial of President Johnson

U.S. SENATE
Impeachment of President
ADMIT THE BEARER
APRIL 17TH 1868.

Ulysses S. Grant

Ulysses S. Grant

18TH PRESIDENT
1869–1877

BORN
April 27, 1822
Point Pleasant, Ohio

INAUGURATED AS PRESIDENT
First term: March 4, 1869
Second term: March 4, 1873

AGE AT INAUGURATION
46

PARTY
Republican

FIRST LADY
Julia Boggs Dent

CHILDREN
Frederick Dent
Ulysses Simpson
Ellen Wrenshall
Jesse Root

DIED
July 23, 1885
Mount McGregor,
New York

As the leading Union general, Ulysses S. Grant became a national hero. Three years after the end of the Civil War, he won the presidency in 1868. Unfortunately, Grant proved to be ill suited to the White House. He had no experience in politics and no real desire to use the full powers of his high office.

Unwittingly, he let dishonest people take advantage of him. Scandals involving railroad fraud and whiskey taxes discredited his administration. After eight years, Grant was happy to leave the White House; he said that he felt like a boy let out of school.

GENERAL GRANT
For Grant, the Civil War provided him with the circumstances by which to make something of himself. He had been frustrated in several occupations—soldier, farmer, realtor, store clerk—before becoming a Union general. On the battlefield, Grant soon proved himself to be a military dynamo.

Paper lantern used in Grant's 1868 campaign

Campaign banner

SOLDIERING ON
During his retirement, Grant continued to experience bad luck. In 1884, he lost his entire savings to an unscrupulous investment broker, and a short time later, he was diagnosed with throat cancer. With an old general's steely determination, Grant decided to write his memoirs in order to provide for his family. Working against the clock, he finished his manuscript just one week before he died. His *Personal Memoirs*, written with modesty and humor, became an instant best-seller.

Grant was aged 61 when this photograph was taken; he died two years later.

Grant's wife, Julia Boggs Dent

Grant surrounded by his family, 1883

General Grant with his horse during the Civil War. A shy man, Grant had loved horses since childhood.

Rutherford B. Hayes

Like Ulysses S. Grant (p. 29), Rutherford B. Hayes had been a Union general during the Civil War. In 1877, he won a controversial election by one vote. Congress decided the contest, which left many of Hayes's opponents feeling cheated. They referred to Hayes as "His Fraudulency" and "Rutherfraud" B. Hayes. Hayes proved to be an even-handed but unexceptional president. He was lenient with the Southern states and removed the last remaining federal troops from their midst. By the end of his single term in office, Hayes had managed to win over his critics.

Photograph of Lucy Hayes, 1878

A POLITICAL BARGAIN
Hayes's opponent in the 1876 election was Democrat Samuel J. Tilden (above left). When Tilden lost the election, southern Democrats were so outraged that they threatened to secede. They declared that they would only accept Hayes as president if he agreed to remove federal troops from the South. Hayes agreed.

THE BATTLE OF LITTLE BIG HORN
In 1868, Congress had recognized the Black Hills of South Dakota as sacred to the Sioux and Cheyenne. But when gold was discovered there in the 1870s, the government tried to move the Indians onto reservations. On June 25, 1876, a federal cavalry, led by George A. Custer, attacked the camp of Chief Sitting Bull on the Little Big Horn River in Montana. Custer and his men were outmaneuvered and all killed. The Indian victory was a short-lived one. Federal troops descended on the area and forced them to surrender.

This bust of Hayes, sculpted in 1876, was intended to convince voters that Hayes was a man of substance.

LEMONADE LUCY
Lucy Hayes was a serious-minded First Lady. She was the first president's wife to hold a college degree and was a supporter of the temperance movement. In fact, the White House became famous for its ban on alcoholic drinks, and Lucy became known as "Lemonade Lucy." She also made her mark by hosting the first Easter egg roll at the White House in 1878.

FIRST PHONE
Hayes was the first president to use a telephone in the White House.

Edison telephone, 1879

Little Big Horn River

Former Civil War officer, General George A. Custer

Ceremonial eagle-feather headdress

Sitting Bull, chief of the Sioux nation, who led the Sioux, Cheyenne, and Arapaho warriors against Custer

James A. Garfield

James A. Garfield was the third Civil War general to become president. Yet for the old soldier, the battlefield proved to be a safer place than the president's office. Four months into his term, Garfield was shot by an assassin. As president, he had wanted to reform the civil service system and purge the post office of corruption. Unfortunately, tragedy intervened and he became the second president to be assassinated.

Memorial ribbon bearing Garfield's portrait

The assassin, Charles Guiteau

President Garfield

AN ASSASSIN STRIKES
President Garfield was shot by a man named Charles Guiteau, who was disgruntled because he could not obtain a federal job. Garfield survived for two months after the shooting. Had he lived in a later age, medical science may have saved him. As it was, Garfield died from his gunshot wounds on September 19, 1881.

Rutherford B. Hayes

19TH PRESIDENT
1877–1881
BORN
October 4, 1822, Delaware, Ohio
DIED
January 17, 1893, Fremont, Ohio

James A. Garfield

20TH PRESIDENT
1881
BORN
November 19, 1831, Orange Township, Ohio
DIED
September 19, 1881, Elberon, New Jersey

Chester A. Arthur

21ST PRESIDENT
1881–1885
BORN
October 5, 1830, North Fairfield, Vermont
DIED
November 18, 1886, New York City, New York

Chester A. Arthur

No one expected Chester A. Arthur ever to become president, but when Garfield was assassinated he took over the nation's highest office. Arthur continued to surprise his friends once he entered the White House. For years, he had been a "spoilsman," which meant that he had been given political jobs in return for his loyalty to the "Stalwarts" of the Republican Party. As president, Arthur's attitude changed. He now believed that politicians should earn federal jobs based on their merits. In 1883, Garfield signed the Pendleton Act, which established the Civil Service Commission. Under the new commission, job seekers had to pass exams before being admitted into the civil service. Arthur was not nominated for a second term by the Republicans.

Chester A. Arthur was a fashionable dresser and was the first president to hire a valet.

A Chinese worker flees from a gang of Irishmen.

Of the 200 U.S. soldiers who followed Custer into battle, not one survived.

CURB ON IMMIGRATION BEGINS
During Arthur's term of office, racial tension in California between the Chinese and Irish communities was a continuing problem. In a time of economic hardship, both groups of workers were competing for the lowest-paid jobs, leading to street fighting in San Francisco. In 1882, Congress passed the Chinese Exclusion Act, which prevented Chinese immigration for ten years.

Grover Cleveland

Grover Cleveland was the only president to serve two terms that did not run consecutively. He was ousted from office in 1889 by Benjamin Harrison, but returned to the White House as president four years later. President Cleveland was known to be honest and hardworking. At times he even answered his own telephone. He believed in "hands-off" government and refused to favor individual groups. For instance, he vetoed what he thought were unnecessary pension bills for Civil War veterans. Cleveland vetoed more legislation than any president before him, earning the nickname "Old Veto." A severe economic depression—the Panic of 1893— plagued Cleveland's second term. Although distressed by the plight of the unemployed, Cleveland did not believe the government should intervene. He was unable to restore the nation's economy and was forced to use federal troops to suppress labor unrest. Cleveland failed to win a third nomination.

Sheet music of Cleveland's wedding march

WHITE HOUSE WEDDING
A highlight of Cleveland's first term was his marriage to Frances Folsom, the daughter of his former law partner, Oscar Folsom. At 21, Frances became the youngest First Lady. She was 28 years younger than Cleveland, and their marriage caused quite a stir. The charming and beautiful First Lady became immensely popular, and her image was soon being used in all kinds of advertising campaigns.

THE MAN OF DESTINY
The son of a poor Presbyterian minister, Grover Cleveland received little formal education, but became a successful lawyer through diligence and determination. In 1881, he was elected mayor of Buffalo, New York, where he made his name as a reformer. A year later, he became governor of New York state. The Democrats were impressed with Cleveland's integrity and nominated him for president in 1884.

Federal troops battle with railroad workers.

THE PULLMAN RAILROAD STRIKE
In 1894, Cleveland sent federal troops to break up a strike by railroad workers at the Pullman Palace Car Company in Chicago. The strike, the result of a pay cut, was interfering with the delivery of the mail. Cleveland had the strike leader arrested and the workers were forced to accept lower wages.

Cleveland campaign banner

Grover Cleveland

22ND PRESIDENT
1885–1889
24TH PRESIDENT
1893–1897
BORN
March 18, 1837, Caldwell, New Jersey
DIED
June 24, 1908, Princeton, New Jersey

Benjamin Harrison

23RD PRESIDENT
1889–1893
BORN
August 20, 1833, North Bend, Ohio
DIED
March 13, 1901, Indianapolis, Indiana

William McKinley

25TH PRESIDENT
1897–1901
BORN
January 29, 1843, Niles, Ohio
DIED
September 14, 1901, Buffalo, New York

Benjamin Harrison

Benjamin Harrison's roots were well-grounded in American history. His grandfather, William Henry Harrison (p. 19), was the ninth president and his great-grandfather signed the Declaration of Independence. Harrison was a gifted public speaker, but did not like to engage in small talk. Those who met him often found him cold and aloof. In matters of policy, Harrison supported the Sherman Antitrust Act of 1890, which was designed to regulate big business and eliminate unfair practices such as monopolies. At the same time, though, Harrison signed the McKinley Tariff Act. This protected big business from foreign competition by placing high tariffs on imported goods. The result was a general rise in prices that did little for the Republican Party's popularity. In foreign affairs, Harrison strengthened the navy with a view to expanding U.S. influence in Central America and the Pacific, notably in Hawaii.

IMMIGRATION
In 1892, the government opened Ellis Island in New York to process the millions of immigrants who were arriving in the United States from Europe. Most new immigrants worked in the lowest-paid jobs and suffered hardship in their workplaces. Many workers became hostile to President Harrison and to what they saw as his protection of big business. Harrison was voted out of office in 1892.

Harrison was nicknamed the "Human Iceberg."

William McKinley

During the Civil War (p. 26), the young William McKinley served under Rutherford B. Hayes (p. 30), who later became president. In 1896, McKinley himself was elected to America's highest office. Like his recent predecessors, McKinley favored a "hands-off" approach to economic affairs, and big business went unchecked. McKinley is best remembered for his foreign policy successes. In 1898, he was persuaded to help the Cubans win their independence from Spain. The Spanish were defeated in a matter of months. By the Treaty of Paris in 1898, the United States acquired Guam, Puerto Rico, and the Philippine Islands. That same year, it also annexed Hawaii. Under McKinley, the nation became a global power.

Pictures of McKinley looking as dour as an undertaker give quite the wrong impression. He was a warm and friendly man who charmed those around him.

ASSASSIN SHOOTS MCKINLEY
On September 6, 1901, William McKinley was shot by an anarchist in Buffalo, New York. Eight days later, the president died from his gunshot wounds.

The assassin hid his revolver underneath a bandage on his hand.

President McKinley's Republican running mate in the 1900 election campaign was the then governor of New York, Theodore Roosevelt (p. 34).

Theodore Roosevelt

WHEN WILLIAM MCKINLEY was assassinated in 1901, Theodore Roosevelt became the youngest president of the United States at the age of 42. Roosevelt was well qualified for the job. Previously a writer and a cowboy, he had also held important political posts, and he was full of energy and idealism. As president, Roosevelt wanted all Americans to have a "square deal," and he fearlessly set about redressing the balance between rich business interests and the needs of workers. He is remembered by many for having inspired the teddy bear.

Medal celebrating Roosevelt's inauguration

TRIUMPHANT INAUGURATION DAY
During his first term, Roosevelt hugely enjoyed being president and he was anxious to continue. He was aware, though, that he had not been elected as the chief executive. Any doubts he had about his popularity were dispelled in 1904 when he was reelected with a massive majority.

A ROUGH RIDER
When the Spanish-American War began in 1898, Roosevelt was serving as assistant secretary of the navy. In his typically energetic way, he immediately resigned and made arrangements to go to Cuba—then struggling to become independent of Spain—to join in the fighting. He raised a volunteer cavalry regiment called the Rough Riders and, in July, led a charge up Cuba's San Juan Hill. The Spanish surrendered soon thereafter and Roosevelt became a hero.

THE WHITE HOUSE GANG
Roosevelt's colorful First Family often caused mayhem at the White House. The wild younger sons were nicknamed the White House Gang by the press. They overran the executive mansion with a menagerie of pets and enjoyed sliding down the central staircase on metal trays. Roosevelt's popular elder daughter Alice enjoyed scandalizing the public. Her father is reported to have said: "I can be President of the United States or I can control Alice. I cannot possibly do both."

A born rebel, Alice Roosevelt kept a pet snake and liked to smoke in public.

Edith Roosevelt presided over her eccentric family with calm and patience.

President Theodore Roosevelt with his family, 1903

Protection for the workers

Roosevelt was an idealistic president who believed that ordinary Americans should be protected against the power of industrialists. When coal miners in Pennsylvania went on strike for higher wages in 1902, Roosevelt threatened to seize the mines unless the owners agreed to arbitration. He invited both sides to Washington to discuss their differences. The miners proceeded to win many of their demands.

Banner portrays Roosevelt as the protector of labor.

Cartoon shows John D. Rockefeller, head of the powerful Standard Oil Trust, about to swallow up the Earth.

ROOSEVELT

PROTECTION.

Theodore Roosevelt

26TH PRESIDENT
1901–1909

BORN
October 27, 1858
New York City, New York

INAUGURATED AS PRESIDENT
First term: September 14, 1901
Second term: March 4, 1905

AGE AT INAUGURATION
42

PARTY
Republican

FIRST LADY
Edith Kermit Carow

CHILDREN
Alice Lee
Theodore
Kermit
Ethel Carow
Archibald Bulloch
Quentin

DIED
January 6, 1919
Oyster Bay,
New York

TEDDY THE CRUSADER
Roosevelt became known as the "Trust Buster" for his crusade to stop the unfair practices of big business. In some industries, such as tobacco, oil, steel, and the railroads, businesses had formed trusts to keep prices high. These trusts also forced small companies out of business and paid low wages to workers. Roosevelt used legislation to curb the powers of trusts.

The whistle was placed over the teeth. The wearer blew through a small gap in the middle.

TEDDY'S TEETH

EQUALITY

A DINNER INVITATION
Theodore Roosevelt believed in racial equality, and was the first president to invite an African American to dinner at the White House. This 1901 lithograph celebrates his meeting with Booker T. Washington, principal of the Tuskegee Institute in Alabama and a renowned African American educator.

TRADEMARK GRIN
Roosevelt was famous for his good humor and broad grin. This novelty whistle in the shape of "Teddy's teeth" was designed for the campaign trail. The advertisement describes it as "just the thing for parades, carnivals, street fairs, political meetings, and campaign clubs."

Continued on next page

PROTECTING THE ENVIRONMENT

A farsighted environmentalist, Roosevelt believed that the American land as well as trees, animals, birds, and fish were resources not to be squandered but maintained properly in the interests of the nation. He established the first federal wildlife refuge in 1903. By executive order, he preserved millions of acres of national forest and established five national parks.

Roosevelt stands with other conservationists in front of the "Grizley Giant" redwood in California.

This cuddly brown "Teddy's bear" quickly became known as the teddy bear, beloved by children ever since.

TEDDY'S BEAR

On a hunting trip in 1902, Roosevelt refused to shoot a captured black bear. The cartoonist Clifford Berryman made this sketch of the incident for the *Washington Post*. Soon after, "Teddy's bears" were being sold as toys.

This photograph of Roosevelt in his riding clothes captures the restless energy of a man with many interests who was seldom idle.

The great outdoors man

Roosevelt had a passion for the great outdoors. He loved to go on hunting trips and safaris. At this time, hunting wild animals was accepted as a manly sport. Roosevelt's home on New York's Long Island was full of his hunting trophies. As president, he also created the first four federal game reserves.

Roosevelt's leather cowboy chaps

ONCE A COWBOY

Roosevelt was once a sickly boy plagued by asthma. Yet he became a lifelong believer in strenuous exercise. After the death in 1884 of his first wife, Alice Lee, he went west and became a cowboy in the Dakota Badlands. After two years, he moved back to New York, a much tougher and fitter man.

William H. Taft

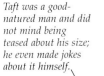

Taft was a good-natured man and did not mind being teased about his size; he even made jokes about it himself.

Wᴇɪɢʜɪɴɢ ᴏᴠᴇʀ 300 ᴘᴏᴜɴᴅs, William H. Taft had the distinction of being the largest president. A special bathtub had to be installed for him at the White House. Compared to Theodore Roosevelt, Taft appeared to be a lackluster president. Yet he continued Roosevelt's progressive policies and initiated more antitrust suits than the Trust Buster Roosevelt himself. Taft's administration also saw the establishment of the federal postal-savings system and the adoption of the Sixteenth Amendment, which allowed for the collection of personal income taxes.

Taft (left) on a diplomatic mission to Japan as Roosevelt's secretary of war, 1905

William H. Taft

27TH PRESIDENT
1909–1913

BORN
September 15, 1857
Cincinnati, Ohio

INAUGURATED AS PRESIDENT
March 4, 1909

AGE AT INAUGURATION
51

PARTY
Republican

FIRST LADY
Helen (Nellie) Herron

CHILDREN
Robert Alphonso
Helen
Charles Phelps II

DIED
March 8, 1930
Washington, D.C.

FIRST BALL OF THE SEASON
As a boy, Taft loved baseball. He was a good hitter, but because of his size, not a fast base runner. When he became president, Taft decided he would throw the first ball on opening day of the baseball season, creating a new presidential tradition.

Baseball bat

Catcher's mitt and ball

AN EASYGOING MANNER
Here, looking almost like a casual bystander, Taft poses informally on a visit to Japan. Easygoing and gregarious, Taft never tried to be pompous. He would sometimes forget people's names and often fell asleep in Cabinet meetings and at public functions. After the dynamic Roosevelt, Taft failed to impress the public. When Taft and Roosevelt fell out in 1910, much of the press supported Roosevelt. On leaving the White House in 1913, Taft declared it to be "the lonesomest place in the world."

"BILL"

Campaign banner emphasizes the jowly but friendly face of "Big Bill."

Early Model T Ford

A NEW AGE ARRIVES
Times were changing fast. Not only did Taft keep cows on the White House lawn, he became the first president to buy automobiles for the White House.

Woodrow Wilson

THE SON OF A PRESBYTERIAN minister, Woodrow Wilson brought strong moral convictions to the presidency. He proved to be a dynamic reformer in domestic affairs, signing legislation to lower tariffs and to regulate businesses and banks. Yet in foreign matters, Wilson found his idealistic approach less successful. He tried hard to keep his country out of World War I, and when American involvement became inevitable, he worked equally hard for peace. At the end of the war, Wilson helped negotiate the Treaty of Versailles, but he was bitterly disappointed when the Senate rejected it.

Woodrow Wilson was awarded the Nobel Peace Prize for his contribution to world peace.

Woodrow Wilson

28TH PRESIDENT
1913–1921

BORN
December 28, 1856
Staunton, Virginia

INAUGURATED AS PRESIDENT
First term:
March 4, 1913
Second term:
March 5, 1917

AGE AT INAUGURATION
56

PARTY
Democratic

FIRST LADIES
Ellen Louise Axson
(died 1914)

Edith Bolling Galt

CHILDREN
Margaret Woodrow
Jessie Woodrow
Eleanor Randolph

DIED
February 3,
1924
Washington, D.C.

Program of inaugural ceremonies, 1917

Medal commemorating Wilson's 1913 inauguration

THE SECOND FIRST LADY
Edith Wilson, seen here with her husband on the campaign trail in 1916, was Woodrow Wilson's second wife. His first wife, Ellen, died one and a half years into his presidency. Just a year later, Wilson became engaged to Edith amid whispered criticisms about the speed of his remarriage. After Wilson's stroke in 1919, Edith ran the White House. Many senators were dismayed by this "petticoat government," but the Wilsons continued in this way until the 1920 election campaign.

A MAN OF PRINCIPLE
Woodrow Wilson was a former college professor and president of Princeton University. As president of the United States, he found it hard to compromise his high moral principles. He is said to have admitted, "I feel sorry for those who disagree with me." When the Senate refused to agree to the Treaty of Versailles in 1919, Wilson stubbornly set off on a national tour to convince the people that his ideas were right. He was already exhausted from the Paris peace talks, and three weeks into the tour he collapsed. Wilson suffered a severe stroke that was to disable him for the remainder of his presidency.

Los Angeles Examiner

WAR! SAYS WILSON; BIG ARMY WANTED

FIRST OF U.S. ARMED SHIPS IS 'U' VICTIM

500,000 MEN NEEDED AT ONCE; AID TO ALLIES WITHOUT LIMIT

CONGRESS RALLIES TO STIRRING PLEA OF NATION'S CHIEF

LATEST EARLY MORNING NEWS

Here Is American Congress War Declaration Resolution

World War I

When war broke out in Europe in 1914, Wilson adopted a neutral stance and struggled to keep the United States out of the conflict. This proved a difficult task. Germany openly declared that U.S. ships would be attacked if they entered the seas around Great Britain. After strong warnings from Wilson, Germany agreed to accept the neutrality of U.S. shipping. But in 1917, this agreement broke down, and it was discovered that Germany was secretly trying to form an anti-American alliance with Mexico. On April 2, Wilson was forced to ask Congress for a declaration of war. Over a million U.S. troops were sent to Europe. They were to prove a decisive factor in the final collapse of Germany in October, 1918.

Famous World War I army recruitment poster of Uncle Sam

President Wilson

The signing of the Treaty of Versailles, June 28, 1919

THE TREATY OF VERSAILLES

Even before the end of the war, Woodrow Wilson had drawn up the Fourteen Points peace plan, which made proposals for "peace without victory." Wilson wanted to establish a League of Nations to help maintain peace among all countries. At the Paris peace talks in 1919, he personally helped negotiate the Treaty of Versailles. The European negotiators, however, did not always agree with Wilson's lenient views toward Germany and he was forced to make compromises. Wilson was angry when the Senate rejected the treaty.

Children were taken on parades to emphasize their mothers' need to have a say in their children's futures.

Suffragettes carry the Stars and Stripes.

VOTES FOR WOMEN

Suffragette button

A federal agent nails a "Closed" sign to a saloon door.

CLOSED

PROHIBITION ARRIVES

In 1919, the United States officially went dry. Alcohol was seen as the source of all evil by religious groups and as the primary cause of poverty, disease, and crime by progressive groups. The Volstead Act and the Eighteenth Amendment now made the consumption of alcohol illegal. It was the beginning of the Prohibition era, which was to see illegal "speakeasy" bars and gangsters flourish during the following years.

WILSON VOTES FOR WOMEN

President Wilson was firmly behind the women's suffrage movement. Women had been campaigning for the right to vote since the mid-19th century. Wilson's support, along with women's involvement in the war effort, finally turned the tide of public opinion in their favor. In August, 1920, the Nineteenth Amendment became law, granting all female U.S. citizens the right to vote.

Warren G. Harding

Warren G. Harding's campaign theme—"Back to Normalcy"—was a call for Americans to return to a simpler, quieter way of life after World War I. Voters liked it and elected Harding by a wide margin. In keeping with Harding's unassuming nature, he yielded much of his executive power to Congress. It reduced taxes, raised tariffs to record heights, and placed quotas on immigration. Unfortunately, Harding delegated authority to a number of advisers who proved to be dishonest, and scandals sullied his administration. In 1923, before he could be impeached for the wrongdoings of those he had trusted, Harding died suddenly, provoking rumors that he had been murdered.

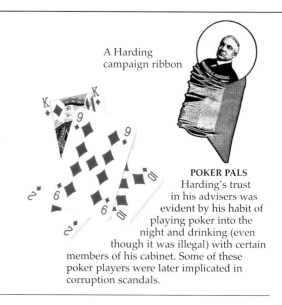

A Harding campaign ribbon

POKER PALS
Harding's trust in his advisers was evident by his habit of playing poker into the night and drinking (even though it was illegal) with certain members of his cabinet. Some of these poker players were later implicated in corruption scandals.

Calvin Coolidge

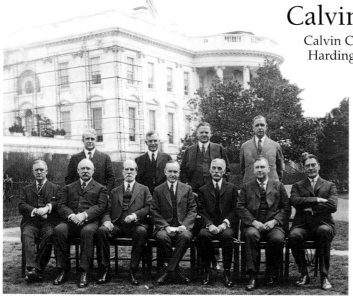

Calvin Coolidge became president upon the sudden death of Warren Harding. Nicknamed "Silent Cal," the taciturn Coolidge talked little and smiled even less. Once, a society lady bet she could make the president say more than three words at dinner. Coolidge replied, "You lose." Coolidge was honest, thrifty, and restrained, and he brought back a sense of trust to the presidency after the murky dealings of Harding's administration. The economy was undergoing a period of great prosperity, and the new president saw no reason to interfere with it, believing that less government was best. It did not matter to most Americans that Coolidge did little to change things. The president enjoyed afternoon naps and allegedly slept more hours in a day than any other president.

STRAIGHT-LACED CAL
Calvin Coolidge (pictured center, with his cabinet, in 1924) was the son of a Vermont shopkeeper. He trained as a lawyer and held several political posts before becoming governor of Massachusetts. Coolidge was a reserved man and said he found meeting new people difficult. But his New England modesty and upright values served him well during his presidency.

AMAZING GRACE
Mrs. Grace Coolidge is pictured here with her tame raccoon named Rebecca. The First Lady was vivacious and enjoyed social gatherings. She was the perfect match for her dour husband and together they formed a happy couple. Their happiness was marred, though, when their youngest son died of blood poisoning in 1924.

Rebecca, the First Lady's pet raccoon

The story of Lindbergh's Atlantic crossing was celebrated in numerous magazines and books.

THE ROARING TWENTIES
Coolidge's "hands-off" approach to the economy encouraged speculation in the stock market and led to a boom time in the 1920s. With lots of money and work, a "live now, pay later" society emerged. Women in particular discovered a new sense of freedom: they cut their hair, wore shorter skirts, and learned how to dance the Charleston.

THE NEW AVIATORS
On May 21, 1927, aviator Charles Lindbergh made the first nonstop solo flight across the Atlantic. Coolidge was so thrilled, that on Lindbergh's return he greeted the pilot with "unrestrained cordiality." The year before, Coolidge had signed the Air Commerce Act to regulate the burgeoning aviation industry.

Herbert Hoover

A self-made businessman and millionaire, Herbert Hoover seemed to be a perfect choice for president. Unfortunately, only months after he took office, the stock market crashed, triggering the Great Depression. Banks ran out of money, businesses went bankrupt, and people lost their jobs. Many people unfairly blamed Hoover for the disaster. Hoover tried hard to rally the nation by making confident speeches, but he did not feel that it was the government's responsibility to provide welfare relief. Although he eventually gave banks and businesses federal loans, he refused to help the destitute.

1928 Hoover button

Warren G. Harding

29TH PRESIDENT
1921–1923
BORN
November 2, 1865, Bloomington Grove, Ohio
DIED
August 2, 1923, San Francisco, California

Calvin Coolidge

30TH PRESIDENT
1923–1929
BORN
July 4, 1872, Plymouth Notch, Vermont
DIED
January 5, 1933, Northampton, Massachusetts

Herbert Hoover

31ST PRESIDENT
1929–1933
BORN
August 10, 1874, West Branch, Iowa
DIED
October 20, 1964, New York City, New York

THE STOCK MARKET CRASH
Fueled by unrestrained speculation, the great stock market crash of October 29, 1929, caused a violent downward spiral in the American economy. Stock prices plummeted and many businesses were ruined. The day of the crash became known as "Black Tuesday."

Ticker tape

In 1929 news of the stock market collapse came by ticker-tape machine.

MOST LIKELY TO SUCCEED
Despite being orphaned as a child, Herbert Hoover became a wealthy mining engineer. During and after World War I, he served as an energetic administrator of food and humanitarian aid in Europe and at home. The voters of 1928 saw Hoover as an American success story. Four years later, in the midst of a deepening depression, Americans lost faith and did not reelect him.

Button urges voters to reelect Hoover in the 1932 election.

A shantytown of makeshift homes. Such settlements became known as Hoovervilles.

SPEED UP RECOVERY RE-ELECT HOOVER KEEP HIM ON THE JOB

Franklin D. Roosevelt

FRANKLIN D. ROOSEVELT became president in the midst of the Great Depression. To bring the country out of its economic misery, Roosevelt had the courage to implement revolutionary programs of aid for businessmen, farmers, bankers, workers, and the unemployed alike. Roosevelt's personal history meant he could empathize with the disadvantaged. He became a victim of polio in middle age and was unable to walk unaided for the rest of his life. His concern for the nation's underprivileged was shared by his wife, Eleanor.

ELEANOR ROOSEVELT
Eleanor married Franklin Roosevelt in 1905. She became First Lady with the intention of being "plain, ordinary Mrs. Roosevelt," but she was soon involved in the plight of the poor. She drew her husband's attention to their needs. Her works of goodwill gave inspiration to Americans everywhere.

Like thousands of others, this destitute farm laborer set off on the road with his family looking for new work.

THE POOR AND HUNGRY
Scenes such as the one pictured above became commonplace as the Great Depression deepened. The situation was made worse by severe drought in the Great Plains states, which created dust bowl conditions. Millions of ordinary Americans suddenly had no work or money. Roosevelt pledged to help them.

Cushion cover with anti-Prohibition message

PROHIBITION ENDS
In 1933, the 21st Amendment ended Prohibition. Most Americans were thankful. The law had led to illicit bootlegging, smuggling, and the rise of gangsters.

A NEW DEAL FOR ALL
Roosevelt called his program of aid and reform the New Deal, and one of his first goals was to put people back to work. He was concerned with helping what he called the forgotten man; that is, the ordinary worker who was unemployed and starving. He set about establishing federal programs for work projects and financial aid—solutions President Hoover (p. 41) had refused to contemplate.

Sheet music for the rousing New Deal March

FIRST FRIEND
Roosevelt's black Scottie dog, Fala, accompanied the president everywhere and soon became a national celebrity.

ROOSEVELT TALKS TO THE NATION
On the eve of the new president's inauguration in 1933, the nation's banking system collapsed. In a memorable speech, Roosevelt promised to deal with the crisis at hand, announcing: "The only thing we have to fear is fear itself." He then closed all the banks. In the first of many "fireside chat" radio broadcasts, he urged people to stop hoarding cash and put it back into the banks. Encouraged by his confident tone, an anxious nation responded.

Reassuring radio broadcasts became an important aspect of Roosevelt's appeal.

In the 1930s, radio was the fastest way of communicating important news to the nation.

Continued on next page

Continued from previous page

Dr. Win-the-War

In 1940, Franklin Roosevelt won a historic third term. No president before had been in office longer than eight years. Roosevelt's leadership was still needed to pull America out of the Depression. Then on the heels of one crisis came another—World War II. Ironically, the war effort was to put an end to the country's economic problems. The United States entered the war in December, 1941, after Japan attacked the U.S. naval base at Pearl Harbor. During the next four years, as commander-in-chief, Roosevelt set up programs for raising and training the millions of men and women needed for the armed forces. With the Allied leaders, Winston Churchill of Great Britain and Joseph Stalin of the Soviet Union, Roosevelt helped plan strategies that would ultimately lead to the defeat of Germany, Italy, and Japan. In 1944, he won reelection so that he could see the war through to its successful end. The war, though, had taken its toll on Roosevelt's health. He died in April, 1945, a month before the German surrender.

With the start of hostilities, Roosevelt took on a new public persona. He declared that "Dr. New Deal" had to become "Dr. Win-the-War."

PEARL HARBOR
On December 7, 1941, Japanese bombers carried out a surprise attack on the U.S. naval and army air bases at Pearl Habor in Hawaii. More than 2,300 servicemen were killed, 1,300 wounded, and 1,000 unacccounted for. The attack also destroyed 18 U.S. ships and more than 200 aircraft. The government was caught off-guard and ill-prepared. President Roosevelt now brought the United States into World War II behind the Allies in Europe and opened up a new front in the Pacific against the Japanese.

U.S.S. Shaw explodes as it is hit by a Japanese bomb in Pearl Harbor

Albert Einstein became a U.S. citizen and professor at Princeton University in 1940.

THE MANHATTAN PROJECT
In August, 1939, President Roosevelt received a letter from the German scientist Albert Einstein. It warned him that Germany might be developing an atomic bomb. At first, Roosevelt did not act upon the warning, but after Pearl Harbor, Roosevelt set up a research project and allocated it two billion dollars. It was code-named the "Manhattan Project" because most of the early work took place at Columbia University in Manhattan. On July 16, 1945, U.S. scientists detonated the world's first atomic bomb near Alamogordo, in the New Mexican desert.

This statue at Arlington Cemetery, Virginia, is based on the famous 1945 photograph by Joe Rosenthal. It symbolizes the triumph, bravery, and sacrifice of American marines in World War II.

THE HOME FRONT

Once America had entered World War II, millions of men and women were needed to serve in the armed forces. On the home front, this left many jobs to be filled. The government launched poster campaigns urging U.S. citizens to work for the war effort. Roosevelt put his energy into getting the nation's factories to retool for war production.

WE ARE NOW IN THIS WAR
We are all in it all the way

Every single man, woman and child is a partner in the most tremendous undertaking of our American history. We must share together the bad news and the good news, the defeats and the victories—the changing fortunes of war.

(President Roosevelt, Address to the Nation, December 9, 1941)

This poster contains the words of one of Roosevelt's morale-boosting speeches.

DEFEND AMERICAN FREEDOM
ITS EVERYBODY'S JOB

The image of Uncle Sam was used to encourage new recruits into the war industry.

The Stars and Stripes was raised by marines over the Pacific island of Iwo Jima after one of the last great battles of the war.

The Big Three at Tehran, Iran, in November, 1943

Joseph Stalin

Franklin D. Roosevelt

Winston Churchill

THE BIG THREE

In November, 1943, Roosevelt met with the Allied leaders Winston Churchill, prime minister of Great Britain, and the Soviet Union's premier, Joseph Stalin. The "Big Three" discussed their strategy for the forthcoming joint invasion of German-occupied France. Stalin was anxious for this to happen soon to take the pressure off the Russian front. In reality, the D-Day invasion would not take place until June 6, 1944. Organized by General Dwight Eisenhower (p. 48), it was a success, and led to the liberation of France and the final defeat of Germany in 1945.

Many believed Roosevelt should not run for a fourth term. This Democratic Party campaign item stresses his suitability for carrying on.

FDR FREEDOM
4 R FOUR FREEDOMS
RE-ELECT ROOSEVELT

THE DIFFERENCE
between the
DEMOCRATS
AND
REPUBLICANS
IS
12 YEARS OF EXPERIENCE

VICTORY IN THE PACIFIC

A small but strategically placed island in the Western Pacific, Iwo Jima was the scene of one of the Pacific war's hardest-fought battles in February, 1945. Almost 7,000 U.S. servicemen were lost in the four-day struggle to gain control of the island. Japan finally surrendered to the United States on August 14, 1945.

Harry S. Truman

Harry S. Truman

33RD PRESIDENT
1945–1953

BORN
May 8, 1884
Lamar, Missouri

INAUGURATED AS PRESIDENT
First term: April 12, 1945
Second term: January 20, 1949

AGE AT INAUGURATION
60

PARTY
Democratic

FIRST LADY
Elizabeth (Bess) Virginia Wallace

CHILDREN
Margaret

DIED
December 26, 1972
Kansas City, Missouri

FRANKLIN ROOSEVELT'S (p. 42) sudden death in 1945 put Vice President Harry S. Truman in the White House with global decisions to make. The war in Europe was drawing to a close, but the Pacific war still needed a swift resolution. The Japanese refused to surrender, and Truman did not want to risk the lives of U.S. servicemen in an invasion. Ultimately, Truman ordered two atomic bombs to be dropped on Japan. Within days, the war was over. Peacetime brought new challenges. Truman now faced such problems as how to educate and train millions of returning troops. In his Fair Deal initiative, he proposed national medical insurance and a civil rights bill, but both were defeated in Congress.

THE TRUMANS AT HOME
Although he met his future wife at Sunday school when he was six, Truman and "Bess" Wallace did not marry until 1919 when they were in their thirties. They had a daughter, Margaret, who attempted to launch a singing career. Here, Truman is seen in a relaxed holiday mood with his wife (left) and daughter (right) giving information for a census.

THE MAN FROM INDEPENDENCE
Franklin Roosevelt was a hard act to follow and Truman, a plain-spoken former haberdasher from Independence, Missouri, sometimes appeared brash in comparison. One of Truman's favorite sayings was: "If you can't stand the heat, get out of the kitchen." He also had a sign on his desk that read, "The Buck Stops Here." Truman knew he had difficult decisions to make as president and he shouldered the burden with determination.

A mushroom-shaped cloud of smoke and dust rose five miles above Hiroshima.

President Truman   George C. Marshall

DROPPING THE BOMB

On August 6, 1945, the U.S. bomber *Enola Gay* dropped an atom bomb over the city of Hiroshima, Japan. At least 100,000 people were killed instantly. That day, Truman wrote, "We have discovered the most terrible bomb in the history of the world."

THE TRUMAN DOCTRINE

At the end of World War II, Stalin (p. 44) established communist governments in Eastern European countries in order to protect the Soviet Union. Truman became deeply concerned about the spread of communism. In 1947, he announced his Truman Doctrine, which promised U.S. support to all countries fighting communists. Later that year, Secretary of State George Marshall proposed the Marshall Plan to provide cash grants to the war-ravaged European countries. Stalin denounced the aid as a capitalist plot. The Cold War between the United States and the Soviet Union had begun.

1948 election campaign poster

★ BEAT HIGH PRICES ★

ELECT **HARRY S. TRUMAN** PRESIDENT ★ ALBEN W. BARKLEY ★ VICE-PRESIDENT

Against the odds, Truman was reelected in 1948, beating the favorite, Governor Thomas Dewey of New York.

THE BERLIN AIRLIFT

In April, 1948, the Soviet Union formed a blockade around Berlin, Germany. The Soviets wanted to bring an end to the continuing presence of Allied troops in that city. Truman immediately ordered essential supplies to be airlifted to Berlin. A constant stream of U.S. and British supply planes enabled the Berliners to survive until the blockade was lifted in May, 1949.

Berlin children watch as an airplane brings in vital supplies.

U.S. troops on the move in Korea

THE KOREAN WAR

When communist North Korea attempted to seize control of South Korea in June, 1950, fears of the spread of communism led Truman to send American troops into a country on the other side of the world. General Douglas MacArthur had orders to liberate South Korea. But when he invaded north across the border, this angered the Chinese communist government, which sent vast numbers of troops into action. This war was to drag on until 1953.

Dwight D. Eisenhower

THE AMERICAN PEOPLE liked "Ike." Dwight D. Eisenhower's eight years in the White House were years of peace and prosperity for most Americans. Eisenhower brought an end to the Korean War in 1953. He also attempted to improve relations with the Soviet Union by organizing a series of cultural exchanges with premier Nikita Khrushchev. These ended, though, when a U.S. spy plane was shot down in Soviet air space. In domestic affairs, Eisenhower was forced to use federal troops to end the segregation of white and black Americans, stating, "There must be no second-class citizens in this country."

LIKABLE IKE
"I Like Ike" became one of the most memorable campaign slogans of the 1950s. Eisenhower's ready smile and relaxed personality ensured his landslide victory in the presidential election of 1953.

ALL-AMERICAN FIRST LADY
Mamie Eisenhower was popular with the voters, and her image as an all-American wife and mother was used to promote her husband as a devoted family man. Although Mamie limited her public appearances, her appeal was enduring.

"I Like Ike" buttons were worn everywhere—even by those who usually voted Democratic.

A 1956 campaign pale for Ike and running mate Richard Nixon.

These "Ike" golf tees from the 1956 Republican campaign promote the president through his favorite sport.

Dwight D. Eisenhower

34TH PRESIDENT
1953–1961

BORN
October 14, 1890
Denison, Texas

INAUGURATED AS PRESIDENT
First term: January 20, 1953
Second term: January 21, 1957

AGE AT INAUGURATION
62

PARTY
Republican

FIRST LADY
Marie (Mamie)
Geneva Doud

CHILDREN
Doud Dwight
John Sheldon

DIED
March 28, 1969
Washington, D.C.

GOLFING PRESIDENT
Eisenhower loved to play golf. He had a putting green and driving range built on the White House grounds, and could often be seen there practicing his swing. Some senators thought the president spent a little too much time trying to lower his handicap.

Eisenhower shakes hands with his five-year-old grandson David on a Georgia golf course.

THE McCARTHY HEARINGS

In the 1950s, the United States was obsessed by fears of communist infiltration. President Truman (p. 46) had ordered an investigation of the government, and this continued under Eisenhower. Senator Joseph McCarthy of Wisconsin became notorious for carrying out communist "witch-hunts" in the State Department. His false allegations ruined many innocent people. Ultimately, McCarthy was himself ruined by his own slanders.

Senator McCarthy chuckles over an anti-McCarthyist advertisement in 1954.

Black students run the gauntlet of an angry mob as they try to enter their new school.

The World War II general

Dwight D. Eisenhower was a good student at West Point, but not a great one. Few would have predicted that he would go so far. During World War II, he was selected to lead the European Theater of Operations. His successful invasions of North Africa, Sicily, and Italy led to his appointment as Supreme Allied Commander in Europe. He organized the famous D-Day landings in northern France in June, 1944. After the war, Eisenhower became chief of staff, the army's highest military office.

LITTLE ROCK

During Eisenhower's presidency, civil rights became a pressing issue. After the Supreme Court ruled in 1954 that segregating black and white citizens was illegal, cities began desegregating their schools. But in the South there was strong resistance. In 1957, Governor Orval Faubus of Little Rock, Arkansas, called out the state's National Guard to prevent a group of black students from enrolling in an all-white high school in the town. Eisenhower was forced to act. He sent federal troops to make sure that the students were escorted safely to school.

Eisenhower in his general's uniform

Sputnik I

THE SPACE RACE

Americans were amazed when, on October 4, 1957, the Soviet Union launched the first satellite, *Sputnik I*, into space. Until then, American scientists had believed their space technology to be in advance of the Russians'. With Eisenhower's approval, Congress set up a new program to sponsor talented young scientists. The space race between the two nations had begun.

John F. Kennedy

Kennedy and his running mate, Lyndon B. Johnson, both supported the same civil rights goals.

Aᴛ ᴛʜᴇ ᴀɢᴇ ᴏғ 43, John F. Kennedy was the youngest president ever elected. Handsome and witty, he won over the voters in a series of televised preelection debates with Richard Nixon (p. 54). Kennedy brought youth, vigor, and vitality to the White House. As part of his New Frontier program, he proposed civil rights legislation and urban renewal. He founded the Peace Corps, a way for young people to promote goodwill in developing countries. Kennedy also encouraged Americans to conquer the new frontier of space. In 1961, he challenged the Soviet Union to put a man on the moon by the end of the decade. His term of office, though, was to be tragically brief. In 1963, Kennedy was assassinated.

PORTRAIT OF A PRESIDENT
Kennedy was born on May 29, 1917, into a large Irish-American family. His father was millionaire tycoon Joseph P. Kennedy. After graduating from Harvard University in 1940, "Jack" joined the navy. During World War II, he was decorated for heroism.

FIRST LADY OF STYLE
Jacqueline Bouvier married John Kennedy on September 12, 1953. They had three children: Caroline Bouvier, John Fitzgerald, Jr., and Patrick, who died in infancy. "Jackie" Kennedy was attractive and charismatic in her own right, and her stylish wardrobe and elegant refurbishment of the White House brought a new kind of glamour to the presidency.

A NEW ERA
Kennedy became famous for his dynamic speeches. In his memorable inaugural address, he demanded of his fellow Americans: "Ask not what your country can do for you—ask what you can do for your country."

ELECTIONEERING
During his entire political career, Kennedy never lost an election. He enjoyed politicking, and in 1960, he ran for president with characteristic enthusiasm. Touting the slogan, "Let's get this country moving again," Kennedy flew around the United States in his own private airplane, wooing the voters with his confidence and charm.

President Kennedy greets supporters, 1962.

Fidel Castro of Cuba

Nikita Khrushchev

NONVIOLENCE...OUR MOST POTENT WEAPON

MARTIN LUTHER KING

Martin Luther King, Jr.'s, policy of nonviolence attracted huge numbers of supporters to his cause.

THE CUBAN MISSILE CRISIS

When Soviet nuclear missile sites were discovered in Cuba, Kennedy ordered a blockade of the island. For 13 days in October, 1962, the United States and the Soviet Union teetered on the brink of nuclear war. Finally, Soviet premier Nikita Khrushchev backed down. Ten months later, Kennedy signed a treaty with the Soviet Union and Great Britain to limit the testing of nuclear weapons.

"I HAVE A DREAM"

In August, 1963, Martin Luther King, Jr., inspired a whole generation of civil rights activists with a speech advocating justice and equality through nonviolent means. Speaking to over 200,000 marchers in Washington, D.C., King invoked the Declaration of Independence when he announced: "I have a dream that one day this nation will rise up and live out the true meaning of its creed: 'We hold these truths to be self-evident, that all men are created equal.'" Kennedy was a firm supporter of equal rights for African Americans, but his civil rights legislation was not passed until after his death.

Jackie Kennedy's quiet dignity at her husband's funeral moved the hearts of millions of television viewers.

KENNEDY IS KILLED IN DALLAS

On November 22, 1963, President Kennedy was riding in an open limousine through Dallas, Texas, when an assassin opened fire. The president was hit in the head and died a short time later. Police arrested 24-year-old Lee Harvey Oswald for the murder, but he was shot two days later by Jack Ruby while in police custody. President Johnson (p. 52) established the Warren Commission to investigate Kennedy's death. It concluded that Oswald had acted alone, but conspiracy theories have surrounded Kennedy's assassination ever since.

AMERICA MOURNS

A grieving nation watched the televised state burial of John F. Kennedy at Arlington National Cemetery, Virginia, on November 25. Representatives of 93 nations came to pay their respects. Kennedy was president only 1,037 days.

This photograph of John F. Kennedy was taken just moments before he was fatally shot.

John Connally, governor of Texas, was also wounded in the shooting.

Jackie Kennedy was not injured.

John F. Kennedy

35TH PRESIDENT
1961–1963

BORN
May 29, 1917
Brookline, Massachusetts

INAUGURATED AS PRESIDENT
January 20, 1961

AGE AT INAUGURATION
43

PARTY
Democratic

FIRST LADY
Jacqueline Lee Bouvier

CHILDREN
Caroline Bouvier
John Fitzgerald
Patrick Bouvier

DIED
November 22, 1963
Dallas, Texas

Lyndon B. Johnson

LYNDON B. JOHNSON became president under tragic circumstances after the death of John F. Kennedy (p. 50). A big man from Texas, Johnson had grand designs for his country. He declared a "war on poverty" and introduced extensive social legislation. Although he sought to promote racial harmony, race riots flared up in many cities. His presidency also saw escalating protests against U.S. involvement in the Vietnam War. Johnson became so discouraged that he refused to seek reelection.

Mrs. Johnson (left) and Jackie Kennedy (right) look on as Lyndon B. Johnson is sworn in as president within hours of John F. Kennedy's death

JOHNSON'S DREAM
Johnson's dream was to make America a "Great Society," free of racial hatred and poverty. He was described by his opponents as ruthless and abrasive. Yet Johnson succeeded in getting his impressive program of social legislation through Congress. The Civil Rights Act of 1964 banned racial segregation in public places and discrimination in employment. The Voting Rights Act of 1965 outlawed the requirement for citizens to prove that they could read and write before they were allowed to vote. This stipulation had robbed many African Americans of their right to vote.

ALL AMERICANS MOVE FORWARD

THE L.B.J. FAMILY
It was a family tradition that all the Johnsons had the initials L.B.J. Johnson called his dog Little Beagle Johnson. His children were named Lydia Bird and Luci Baines, and the First Lady was affectionately known as Lady Bird, although her real name was Claudia Alta.

Young antiwar protesters taunt the military police outside the Pentagon during a demonstration in October, 1967.

Sheet music for the Great Society March

"We have talked long enough in this country about equal rights. We have talked 100 years or more. It is time to write the next chapter, and write it in the books of law."
—President Johnson
November 27, 1963

Poster promoting Johnson's stand on civil rights

The first U.S. combat troops land at Da Nang, South Vietnam, March 11, 1965

Lyndon B. Johnson

The Vietnam War

When Lyndon Johnson became president, about 16,000 American soldiers were in South Vietnam acting as military advisers to the government. They were trying to stop the communists in the North from taking over the entire country. The aggressive actions of the communists, however, soon led Johnson to order bombing raids. In 1965, he sent combat troops to protect American bases. Yet the conflict only escalated. By 1968, the United States had more than 500,000 troops in Vietnam. With American casualties mounting and no victory in sight, Johnson despaired of finding a quick and honorable end to the war.

Anti-Vietnam War poster of a battered Uncle Sam

PEACE AND PROTEST
"Make love not war" became the rallying cry of America's youth, who were increasingly disenchanted with Johnson's Vietnam War policies. Antiwar protests soon became a mass movement, giving rise to the Sixties' counterculture of hippies and "flower children." The Vietnam War cost Johnson dearly. Voted "Man of the Year" by *Time* magazine in 1964, by 1968, Johnson was reviled.

This 1967 cartoon depicts Johnson in a sick bed with the South Vietnamese leader Ky, who is sucking the president's blood.

Richard M. Nixon

FEW PEOPLE HAVE experienced the highs and lows of politics like Richard Nixon. He was an admirable vice president to Dwight Eisenhower (p. 48) from 1953 to 1961, but lost a close presidential election to John F. Kennedy (p. 50) in 1960. Just when his political career seemed to be over, Nixon was elected president in 1968. He showed a flair for foreign diplomacy, witnessed the lunar landing of 1969, and brought an end to U.S. military involvement in Vietnam. Yet despite all of its successes, Nixon's administration is primarily remembered for the Watergate scandal. Subsequently faced with impeachment, Richard Nixon became the first U.S. president to resign.

NIXON ON HIS WAY UP
After he failed to win either the presidency or the governorship of California, Richard Nixon decided to quit politics in 1962. He moved to New York to practice law. Before long, however, Nixon decided to run as the Republican candidate in the 1968 presidential election.

Nixon inaugural pennants

Mao and Nixon knock a ping-pong ball, and opposing ideologies, back and forth across the table in this political cartoon.

A MATCH FOR MAO
When Nixon sensed a rift between America's Cold War enemies, China and the Soviet Union, he saw an opportunity to forge new links with China. Through his aide, Henry Kissinger, Nixon opened negotiations with Chairman Mao. In 1971, Mao invited the U.S. ping-pong team to China and Nixon went to Beijing for talks with Chinese premier Zhou Enlai. In 1972, Nixon continued this policy of *détente*, or relaxation, by visiting Moscow in the Soviet Union. At the conclusion of this trip, he announced plans for a joint U.S.-Soviet program to limit nuclear arms.

Artist Norman Rockwell claimed Nixon was "the hardest man" he ever painted. He had struggled to portray Nixon's heavy-jowled face in a suitably flattering light.

EARLY DAYS
The son of a California grocer, Nixon graduated from law school in 1937 and practiced law before joining the navy in 1942. Nixon's political career began when he was elected to Congress in 1946. Nixon earned the nickname "Tricky Dick" for his cunning in politics.

Buzz Aldrin photographed on the moon's surface by Neil Armstrong

"THE EAGLE HAS LANDED"
On July 20, 1969, the United States put a man on the moon, fulfilling President Kennedy's 1961 pledge (p. 50). With the now historic words, "One giant step for man, one giant leap for mankind," U.S. astronaut Neil Armstrong left the lunar module *Eagle* and stepped onto the moon's surface. President Nixon spoke with Armstrong and his fellow astronaut Edwin "Buzz" Aldrin during their moon walk while millions of people watched the event on television worldwide.

Richard M. Nixon

37TH PRESIDENT
1969–1974

BORN
January 9, 1913
Yorba Linda, California

INAUGURATED AS PRESIDENT
First term: January 20, 1969
Second term: January 20, 1973

AGE AT INAUGURATION
56

PARTY
Republican

FIRST LADY
Thelma Catherine (Pat) Ryan

CHILDREN
Patricia; Julie

DIED
April 22, 1994, New York, N.Y.

Nixon shakes hands with G.I.s of the First Infantry Division during his tour of Vietnam in July, 1969.

"An American Tragedy"

IMPEACH NIXON!

Watergate

In June, 1972, five burglars were caught planting bugging devices in the Democratic Party headquarters at the Watergate complex in Washington, D.C. Soon, reports began to circulate that the president might be implicated. During the investigations that followed, Nixon strenuously denied involvement in any illegal activities. However, witnesses later testified that Nixon had directed a cover-up of the Watergate affair and that he also had taped all conversations held in the Oval Office at the White House. Nixon tried everything in his power to avoid handing over the incriminating tapes, but in July, 1974, the tapes were finally heard. Three articles of impeachment were immediately issued against Nixon.

VIETNAM
In a bid to honor his campaign promise to bring the Vietnam War to an end, Nixon decided on a policy of "Vietnamization." This meant withdrawing U.S. combat forces and replacing them with South Vietnamese, while continuing to provide air support and supplies. Nixon also stepped up the bombing of North Vietnam and secretly started bombing enemy bases in neighboring Laos and Cambodia. The United States finally signed a peace agreement with the North Vietnamese in January, 1973, and by March, all U.S. combat troops had been withdrawn from Vietnam.

NIXON RESIGNS
In a press conference in November, 1973, Richard Nixon told the American people, "I am not a crook." Yet it soon became clear that Nixon had been involved in illegal activities. In August, 1974, after a long, hard fight, Nixon was forced to resign or face impeachment proceedings. When he left the White House on August 9, Nixon forced a grin and gave his usual victory salute.

Nixon makes his televised resignation speech.

Gerald R. Ford

GERALD R. FORD'S RISE to the presidency was historic. Appointed vice president by Richard Nixon (p. 54) after Spiro Agnew stepped down in 1973, Ford was then sworn in as president in 1974 when Nixon resigned. He became the first president to hold office without ever having been elected by the people. Ford announced: "Our long national nightmare is over" and immediately set about restoring credibility to America's highest office. In a controversial gesture to heal the nation (and also to prevent a lengthy trial), he pardoned Nixon of any wrongdoing. He also offered amnesty to Vietnam War deserters and draft-dodgers.

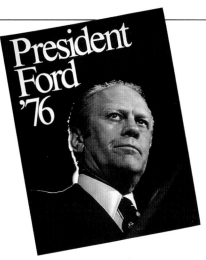

AN EVENTFUL YEAR
A highlight of Ford's two-and-a-half-year presidency was the 1976 Bicentennial celebration of the nation's founding. Later that year, Ford lost the national election to Jimmy Carter.

THE FOOTBALL STAR
Gerald R. Ford went to the University of Michigan, where he enjoyed a dazzling football career. Afterward, in 1941, he graduated in law from Yale University. Ford's nickname was "Mr. Nice Guy," but he also had a reputation for being a patient thinker. Lyndon B. Johnson (p. 52) unkindly remarked that Ford had played too much football without his helmet on.

A BRAVE FIRST LADY
Betty Ford was a charismatic and outspoken First Lady. She was a champion of women's rights and handicapped children. In order to help inform women about breast cancer, she publicized her own mastectomy. After her husband left office, Mrs. Ford bravely admitted to being an alcoholic and dependent on prescription drugs. With treatment, she recovered and went on to help found the Betty Ford Center in California.

Gerald R. Ford

38TH PRESIDENT
1974–1977

BORN
July 14, 1913
Omaha, Nebraska

INAUGURATED AS PRESIDENT
August 9, 1974

AGE AT INAUGURATION
61

PARTY
Republican

FIRST LADY
Elizabeth Anne
Bloomer

CHILDREN
Michael Gerald
John Gardiner
Steven Meigs
Susan Elizabeth

President Ford with his wife, Betty, and their family.

EVACUATION OF SAIGON
The peace treaty negotiated by President Nixon in Vietnam did not last long. In April, 1975, communist forces captured the city of Saigon in South Vietnam. Prior to the invasion, hundreds of American citizens and Vietnamese refugees were airlifted to safety, bringing an end to U.S. involvement in Vietnam.

Jimmy Carter

WHEN AMERICANS voted for Jimmy Carter in 1976, they were voting for change. Burdened by the high cost of living and tired of recent scandal-ridden politics, they saw Carter as a fresh new face in town. A born-again Christian, Carter touted his human decency, while promising to fix the economy. Stemming high inflation, however, proved to be harder than Carter had predicted. Nor could he do much to ease the energy crisis, which was caused by a worldwide oil shortage. Although Carter meant well, Americans soon came to regard him as ineffective.

Carter bumper stickers

Jimmy Carter

39TH PRESIDENT
1977–1981

BORN
October 1, 1924
Plains, Georgia

INAUGURATED AS PRESIDENT
January 20, 1977

AGE AT INAUGURATION
53

PARTY
Democratic

FIRST LADY
Eleanor Rosalynn Smith

CHILDREN
John William
James Earl III
Jeffrey
Amy Lynn

THE PEANUT FARMER
Jimmy Carter grew up near Plains, Georgia, on a peanut farm. After studying nuclear physics, he joined the navy. When his father died, Carter returned to look after the family business.

CARTER DELIVERS CAMP DAVID ACCORD
In 1978, Carter played the role of international peacemaker by hosting peace talks between President Sadat of Egypt and Prime Minister Begin of Israel. After nearly two weeks at Camp David, Maryland, the two leaders signed peace accords. This ended the state of war between the two countries that had existed since 1948. Carter was widely praised for his skill and determination; he had achieved a stunning breakthrough.

CARTER GRAPPLES WITH IRAN
In November, 1979, a group of militant Iranians took the staff of the U.S. embassy in Tehran hostage. The Iranians were angered by continuing U.S. support of the exiled shah of Iran. Carter's negotiations with the Iranian government for the hostages' release failed. In April, 1980, he approved a military rescue mission, but it also failed and eight servicemen were killed. The stalemate made Carter look ineffective in a crisis and shattered his reelection chances. The hostages were finally released in January, 1981, on Carter's last day in office.

Cowboy-style Reagan and Bush belt buckle made for the 1984 campaign

Ronald Reagan

AT 69, RONALD REAGAN was the oldest president to enter the White House. A former movie actor, he became known as the "Great Communicator" because he was completely at ease in front of a television camera. Reagan's plan to boost the economy was to reduce taxes for the rich while cutting back on welfare programs. He believed that by supporting business, prosperity would filter down through all levels of society. Reagan also drastically increased defense spending. Although inflation was reduced, by the end of the 1980s the national debt had doubled. Nevertheless, Reagan remained an extremely popular president.

STAR QUALITY
Ronald Reagan was the son of an Illinois shoe salesman. His first job out of college was as a radio sports announcer. Then, in 1937, he went to Hollywood to work as an actor for Warner Brothers. Reagan made more than 50 movies, including the 1951 comedy *Bedtime for Bonzo*, above.

ASSASSINATION ATTEMPT
Shortly after he took office in 1981, President Reagan was shot by a deranged man. As doctors prepared to remove a bullet from his lung, the president joked, "I forgot to duck." Reagan made a remarkable recovery.

Reagan and Gorbachev pose for photographers in 1986.

Painting of Reagan by Aaron Shikler that appeared on the cover of *Time* magazine in January, 1981

THE COLD WAR THAWS
In 1985 Mikhail Gorbachev became the leader of the Soviet Union and announced a new era of *glasnost* (openness) and *perestroika* (restructuring) in his country's affairs. President Reagan declared, "We can cooperate," and cautiously embarked on arms-control talks. In 1988, both leaders signed the Intermediate-Range Nuclear Forces Treaty, agreeing to limit the arms race.

Moments after this photograph was taken, the Challenger *space shuttle exploded, killing all seven astronauts.*

Nancy Reagan launched a campaign to warn young people against the dangers of drug abuse.

Shuttle disaster

America's space program underwent a huge setback when the *Challenger* space shuttle exploded shortly after liftoff on January 28, 1986. All seven members of the highly publicized flight were killed, including schoolteacher Christa McAuliffe, who had planned to broadcast lessons from space. Reagan's expensive "Star Wars" defense system also received adverse publicity. It was intended to divert nuclear missiles away from the United States using space-based lasers, but years of costly research produced limited results.

Lieutenant Colonel Oliver North arranged the money transfers to the contras. Here he testifies before Congress.

NANCY REAGAN
Born Anne Francis Robbins in New York City in 1923, Nancy Reagan was adopted as a young child and took her stepfather's name, Davis. Later taking the stage name Nancy Davis, she became an actress, making 11 movies in the 1950s. She became Ronald Reagan's second wife in 1952 and helped him build his political career. Although a popular First Lady, Nancy Reagan was criticized for her extravagant tastes and for having too much influence on her husband.

THE IRAN-CONTRA AFFAIR
In November, 1986, a scandal emerged that cast a shadow over Reagan's second term. A foreign press report revealed that the National Security Council had secretly and illegally sold weapons to Iran in an attempt to secure the release of captive American citizens. To make matters worse, the money from the arms deals had been used to aid the anticommunist contras in Nicaragua—despite such aid being outlawed by Congress. In a television broadcast to the nation, President Reagan declared that he knew nothing about these deals, but his credibility suffered.

Ronald Reagan

40TH PRESIDENT
1981–1989

BORN
February 6, 1911
Tampico, Illinois

INAUGURATED AS PRESIDENT
First term: January 20, 1981
Second term:
January 20, 1985

AGE AT INAUGURATION
69

PARTY
Republican

FIRST LADY
Nancy Davis

CHILDREN
Maureen
Michael Edward
Patti Davis
Ronald Prescott

George Bush

FROM THE START, foreign affairs dominated much of George Bush's presidency. In 1989, he ordered troops into Panama to oust the corrupt dictator, General Manuel Noriega. A year later, he was rallying a multinational coalition to force Iraq out of neighboring Kuwait. When the American-led forces decisively won the Persian Gulf war, Bush emerged a popular hero. The collapse of the Soviet Union, ending the Cold War, only strengthened Bush's image as the world's most powerful leader. Yet as unemployment increased and the country went into economic recession, Bush's popularity eroded.

BARBARA BUSH
Barbara Pierce married George Bush in 1945 and they had five children. Mrs. Bush used her role as First Lady to become involved in charitable work. Her efforts on behalf of others earned her respect throughout the country and she became very popular.

President Bush cheers on U.S. troops during the Gulf war.

WIN ONE, LOSE ONE
George Bush was the first vice president to be elected president since Martin Van Buren (p. 18) in 1836. When he ran for reelection in 1992, however, Bush could not convince the voters to stick with a conservative Republican agenda for another four years.

Bush was Ronald Reagan's running mate in 1980 and 1984.

George Bush

41ST PRESIDENT
1989–1993

BORN
June 12, 1924
Milton, Massachusetts

INAUGURATED AS PRESIDENT
January 20, 1989

AGE AT INAUGURATION
64

PARTY
Republican

FIRST LADY
Barbara Pierce

CHILDREN
George Walker
Robin
John Ellis
Neil Mallon
Marvin Pierce

SAVING THE PLANET

Concerns about the environment and global warming became pressing issues in the 1980s. In his 1988 campaign, Bush promised that he would become the environmental president. In 1992, he attended the United Nations Earth Summit in Rio de Janeiro, where he signed the Earth Pledge, which required nations to limit the emission of greenhouse gases, monitor biodiversity, and work toward eco-friendly development. Bush was unwilling, however, to increase financial aid to developing nations in order to help them meet their environmental goals.

Germans from East and West join hands along the Berlin Wall in front of the Brandenburg Gate.

EAST REJOINS WEST AT LAST

On November 9, 1989, East Germans began to tear down the Berlin Wall that had divided East from West Berlin for 28 years. This symbolic event heralded the end of the Cold War. By 1990 Germany was reunified and the communist governments in Eastern Europe had begun to collapse. A friendlier relationship between the Soviet Union and the U.S. ensued. In Bush's words, there was now a "new world order."

The Gulf War

In August, 1990, Iraq's leader, Saddam Hussein, ordered the invasion of his oil-rich neighbor Kuwait. When Saddam refused to withdraw his troops, George Bush coordinated a military coalition of U.S. and allied forces against him. In January, 1991, a sustained bombing campaign—Operation Desert Storm—was launched against Iraq from Saudi Arabia. Six weeks later, the Iraqis were driven out of Kuwait by ground forces. Bush had shown himself as a dynamic world leader.

William Jefferson Clinton

THE FIRST U.S. PRESIDENT to be born after World War II, Bill Clinton knew from a young age that someday he wanted to hold high office. At 32, he was elected governor of Arkansas, becoming the youngest governor-elect in the country. Fourteen years later, he left the governor's mansion for the White House. As president, Clinton enjoyed a time of peace and prosperity. During his first term, he negotiated the successful North American Free Trade Agreement with Canada and Mexico, and secured peace in Haiti by reinstating ousted president Jean-Bertrand Aristide. Clinton failed, though, to have his package of health care reforms passed by Congress. The second term of Clinton's administration was undoubtedly marred by the Monica Lewinsky scandal, but even this failed to diminish Clinton's favorable job-performance ratings in the opinion polls.

THE FIRST FAMILY
Bill Clinton and Hillary Rodham first met at Yale University Law School. They married in 1975 and moved to Little Rock, Arkansas, in 1976 when Clinton was appointed state attorney general. They have one child, Chelsea, who was born in 1980.

A SECOND TERM
Supported by a strong economy, Clinton and his Democratic running mate, Al Gore, were reelected in 1996. Their reelection was not necessarily a foregone conclusion, because in 1994, the Republicans had won control of both the House of Representatives and the Senate.

A FATEFUL ENCOUNTER
In 1963, 16-year-old Bill Clinton was elected as a delegate to a national conference of high school students. Along with others, he was invited to visit the White House. There, he met and shook hands with his hero, President Kennedy (p. 50). This encounter fueled Clinton's ambition to one day become president himself.

FOREIGN AFFAIRS

In July, 1998, President Clinton made a controversial decision to commit U.S. forces to a NATO operation to prevent ethnic cleansing in Kosovo (above). Part of the former Yugoslavia, Kosovo, a region of southern Serbia, was occupied mainly by ethnic Albanians. Thousands of Albanians were forced to flee their homes as Serb soldiers burned villages and killed families. In 1999, Clinton agreed to support a NATO plan of air strikes against Serbia in an attempt to halt the atrocities. The bombing campaign finally forced the Serbs into submission, but a lasting peace in Kosovo remains to be formed.

Clinton gathers his thoughts before making a personal statement to the nation concerning his relationship with Monica Lewinsky.

Clinton confesses

In 1997, Clinton was faced with allegations concerning his relationship with 21-year-old White House intern, Monica Lewinsky. Although Clinton initially denied the allegations, he was eventually forced to admit to a grand jury that he had indeed had an "inappropriate relationship" with Lewinsky. Impeachment proceedings on charges of perjury and obstruction of justice followed in January, 1999. A month later, Clinton was acquitted.

A POLITICIAN IN HER OWN RIGHT
No First Lady has had such an active role in politics as Hillary Rodham Clinton. "If you elect Bill, you get me," she said during the 1992 campaign. Mrs. Clinton was a full-time lawyer with an interest in children's issues before Clinton appointed her to head his task force on health care.

CHICAGO WELCOMES HILLARY

Pin in the shape of Clinton's saxophone

Campaign badge reads: "The cure for the blues."

CLINTON FOR PRESIDENT

RHYTHM AND BLUES
A talented young musician, Bill Clinton was offered several music scholarships when he graduated from high school. Clinton decided to study politics instead of music and attended Georgetown University in Washington, D.C. As president, Clinton has, on occasion, played his saxophone for the public.

Clinton waits in the Map Room of the White House, August 17, 1998

William Jefferson Clinton

42ND PRESIDENT
1993–

BORN
August 19, 1946
Hope, Arkansas

INAUGURATED AS PRESIDENT
First term: January 20, 1993
Second term: January 20, 1997

AGE AT INAUGURATION
46

PARTY
Democratic

FIRST LADY
Hillary Rodham

CHILDREN
Chelsea

Index

Acknowledgements

Dorling Kindersley would like to thank:
The staff of the Smithsonian Institution, Washington, D.C., particularly Beverly Cox at the National Portrait Gallery, Larry Bird and Lisa Kathleen Graddy at the National Museum of American History, and Ellen Nanney and Linda Sheriff at Product Development and Licensing, for making it all happen.

Picture credits
(t = top, b = bottom, l = left, r = right, c = center, a = above)
American Document Company: 5t, 11, 14tl, 24cl, 25cl, 27tc; Associated Press AP: 63bl; Bridgeman Art Library: 6tr, 24b, 27c; Camera Press: 52tr; Dorling Kindersley Picture Library/Wilberforce House, Hull City Museum: 22tl; ET Archive: 5b, 21cl, 30b; Mary Evans Picture Library: 6bl, 9tr, 12cla, bl, 17tl, 31br, 33br, 50tr; Hulton Getty Images: 44bl, c; NASA: 55t; Metropolitan Museum of Art, New York, U.S.A./Bridgeman Art Library: 4c; Peter Newark's Pictures: 6br, 7tl, tc, 10bl, 12-13, 14c, 15tr, 18b, 22tr, cla, br, 23tr, bl, 32cr, 33tl, 35cl, 36tl, 39tr, br, 40bl, bc, br, 42c, 44-5b, 46-7c, 47b, cr, 51tr, 52tl, 53cr, 55cl, 58cl; Popperfoto: 8-9b, 51tl, b, 52-3b, 56br, 62bl, 63tl; Smithsonian Institution: 4tr, 6tl, 7bl, 8cl, bl, 10br, 12tl, tr, 13tr, 14br, 15br, 16cl, 17tr, 18tr, trb, 19tl, br, 23c, 24tr, c, 27cb, cr, br, 28tl, 29tc, ca, cb, 30tl, 31ca, 32t, 33bc, 35br, bl, 36br, 37crb, 38tl, c, 39bc, 40tr, 41tc, crb, 42bc, 43tc, 45tc, tr, br, 48cl, cra, cr, crb, b, 50tl, cr, 51tc, 54tl, cla, clb, 55c, 56tr, 57tc, ca, cb, 58tl, 60ca, cb, 62c, crb, 63trb, c, cb; /Becker Collection: 17br; /Langbourn Washburn: 48t; /Library of Congress: 5cra; /Robert G Myers: 39tl; /National Museum of American History: 4tl, br, 5crb, 7cr, 9tl, 10tl, 12clb, 16tc, tr, 17bl, 19bc, 20tl, 22bl, 28br, 30tr, 32br, 34tla, tlb, tr, 35c, 36c, 38clb, 39bl, 47cl, cra, ca, 52bc, br, 55crb; /National Portrait Gallery: 4-5, 6c, 7cl, br, 8t, 10tr, 14tr, 15tl, c, bl, 16tl, br, 18tl, 19c, bl, 20tr, 20-21b, 21tr, 22cr, 23cl, cr, br, 25bl, 26cl, bl, 26-7b, 27tr, 28tr, cl, b, 29tl, tr, br, bl, 30cl, bl, 31cb, 32bl, 33tr, cl, 34b, 36tl, bl, 37tl, cra, 38tr, b, 39cr, 40tl, cl, 41cl, 46bl, 47tr, 49bl, 53br, 54c, b, 56cl, 57br, 58bl, 60tl; Dorothy Garfein: 42tr; /Charles H. Phillips: 4bl; /Rosalind Solomon: 59br; /George D. Tames: 50, b; /Diana Walker: 60-61lb, 62l; Science & Society Picture Library: 30cr; Topham Picturepoint: 1, 14bl, 25t, 41b, 42-3b, 43cr, 44tl, 45cr, 46cr, 49tl, tr, 53t, 55b, 57cl, bl, 58cr, br, 58-9b, 59tr, c, 60tr, 61c, 62tr, 63tr.
Additional illustration: Alan Reason; additional photography: Tina Chambers, Lynton Gardiner, Dave King, Matthew Ward; index: Chris Bernstein